MAKE IT
MEND IT

AND

MAKE IT AND MEND IT

D&C

David and Charles

www.rucraft.co.uk

CONTENTS

Clare Flynn

Hilary Bruffell

Anne Caborn

Clare O'Brien

Introduction

Make it and Mend it, or MIAMI as we quickly came to call it, was conceived over a long lunch. The four of us were doing a business project together and got talking about our various interests. It turned out that we all loved making things, baking things, growing stuff and fixing stuff. As we shared stories of our latest triumphs and disasters, we began to lament the fact that so many people nowadays don't know how to knit, to sew, to change a plug or to experience eating something they have grown and cooked for themselves. So the idea for MIAMI was born – initially as a kind of 'How to' website to share basic skills. But very quickly we realized it was about much more than that…

The MIAMI way of life is better for you, better for the planet and better for your friends and family – who will soon find themselves on the receiving end of beautiful handmade gifts.

There is no better feeling than being able to say 'I made it' when someone admires something or happily receives it as a gift.

At MIAMI, we believe that human beings were designed to make things. It is wired into our DNA. Yet all those years of the consumer society have caused many of us to lose this capacity and some of us have never even experienced the joy of making something.

Being creative and making things is actually good for us. It builds our self-esteem, helps us feel more capable and in control, reduces depression and generally lifts the spirits. (Hilary has a doctorate in Psychology and assures us this is the case – but anyway we all feel this to be true ourselves.)

Take gardening. Digging, pushing a mower, weeding and carrying soil all use the same muscle groups as lifting

weights in the gym and can increase heart rate, oxygen intake and energy expenditure. Then psychologically, the process of planning your garden can strengthen neural pathways in the brain and increase your memory and hand-eye coordination. Even the soil is good for us – the microbes in it have been found to alleviate depression.

Or knitting? It has a neurochemical effect on the brain, possibly decreasing stress hormones and increasing the feel-good serotonin and dopamine. Not to mention keeping your hands busy when you are trying to quit smoking or stick to a diet.

So whether you choose to bake a loaf, sew a cushion cover, hang some shelves or plant a row of cabbages, you will save money and feel happier and more fulfilled.

And don't imagine that making things means buying lots of expensive materials and equipment. Our favourite projects and many of those in this book, involve our philosophy of 'Thinking outside the bin' – coming up with ideas to re-use, re-style or

re-define things we might otherwise throw away. So old sweatshirts can be turned into a beautiful patchwork quilt, an old fire grate becomes a garden herb planter, and old jam jars are filled with home-made preserves or are turned into tealight holders. And equipment can be bought second hand, borrowed, swapped or hired.

In this book we have collected some of our easy-to-make projects and grouped them by season. We have also thrown in some great ideas for those special occasions like Christmas or Mother's day and shared some top tips and the essential techniques you will need to do them. You will find a host of practical, fun ideas to keep you busy right through the year.

To make more of life – make it and mend it!

Equipment and materials

Sewing

You don't have to buy a purpose-built sewing box: a good stout box, a lidded storage box or a series of small open bins will do fine.

You will acquire more items as time goes on, but the following are a good start.

A pair of fabric scissors

It is definitely worth spending a bit more money on some good quality shears. Don't use these in the kitchen or for cutting paper – keep them for fabric – and don't let the kids get their hands on them.

Pinking shears

These are used to trim fabrics and stop seams fraying so you don't need an overlocker on your sewing machine.

Embroidery scissors

A nice pair with a fine sharp point is perfect for fiddly cutting and getting into awkward spots.

Threads

Your thread collection will grow as you buy different threads to match fabrics, but start off with a basic range of commonly used colours such as black, white, cream, grey, navy, beige; then build from there. Or get a multipack with lots of colours.

Fabric tape measure

With both metric and imperial measures if possible.

Needles and pins

A set of multipack needles with different eyes, plus a couple of embroidery needles.

Every crafter needs a pincushion. Make yourself one and fill it with straight pins with coloured ends as they are easy to handle and harder to lose.

Seam ripper

Essential for unpicking – particularly if you are upcycling an existing item such as a sweatshirt (see our **No Sweat Quilt** and **Hot Water Bottle Cover** projects).

Sewing machine

You can make all the sewing projects in this book by hand if you are prepared to spend a bit longer – but if you want to sew frequently get your hands on a machine. Before you buy one, ask among friends or family if they could let you borrow one for a short time so you can get used to using one before committing to buying.

Don't be frightened of the sewing machine – it is your friend! Get someone to show you the ropes – or join a local sewing class. Plus there are a lot of free tuition videos to be found online.

Iron and ironing board

Essential kit for pressing seams and iron-on webbing.

Fabric stash

Start collecting bits of old fabric. Rummage about in the remnants section of fabric shops, wait for sales, cut up old clothes and save old curtains. Keep leftover fabric when you finish a project. Even small pieces can be useful.

It is also worth keeping some felt in your stash – you can buy a pack of mixed colours for not very much. For some of the projects in this book you will need polyester wadding (batting) or stuffing. A bag of toy stuffing is a useful standby.

Iron-on interfacing

Incredibly useful for stiffening or strengthening fabrics.

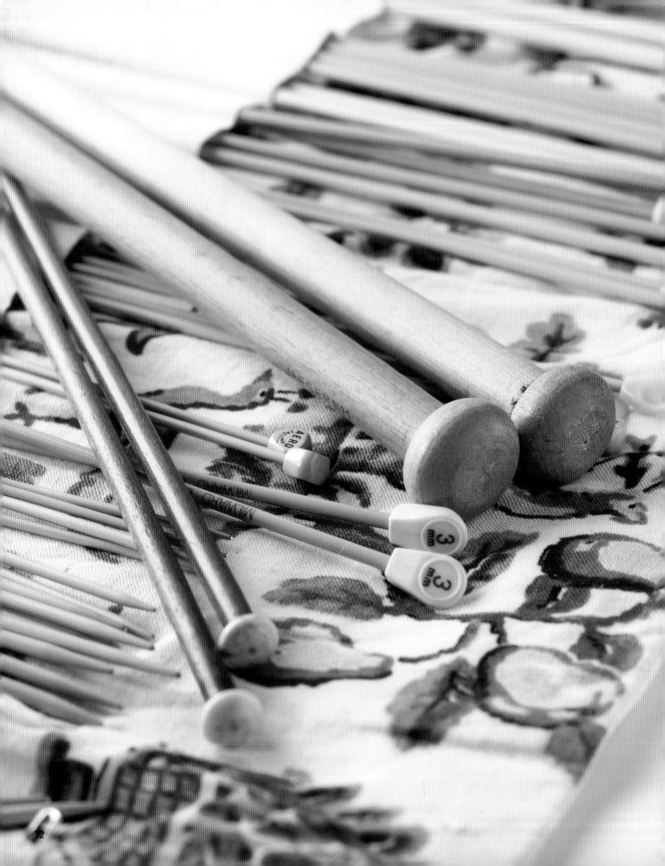

Knitting

Knitting needles
These come in a vareity of sizes and types. Just build up a collection over time as you use patterns. For the **Draught Excluder** project in this book you will need a pair of 6mm (US size 10) ones.

Darning or tapestry needle
You will need a big thick needle to sew up finished articles.

Scissors
Worth having a dedicated pair of small scissors to keep in your knitting bag so you don't have to run round the house trying to find them at that crucial moment.

Craft

Cutting mat
Use this for sewing and DIY too. It keeps your table or worktop protected and is vital for cutting card with sharp craft knives.

Scalpel knife
Essential for cutting card more precisely than scissors can. Use on the cutting mat.

Glues
It is a good idea to have some spray adhesive glue – great for card making (but wear a mask and spray outdoors) – and some PVA glue. If you do a lot of crafting, then a glue gun is a good investment.

Acrylic paint
Again you can build a collection, but start out with blue, red, yellow and white.

Coloured card and tissue paper
It is worth keeping a small stock on hand. Also card blanks – once you start making your own greeting cards you won't stop!

Bits and pieces
It is amazing what a difference some embellishments can make to a project. Start building up your own treasure trove of bits and pieces – stones from broken jewellery, beads, odd buttons, bits of ribbon, scraps of fabric, old postcards and wrapping paper.

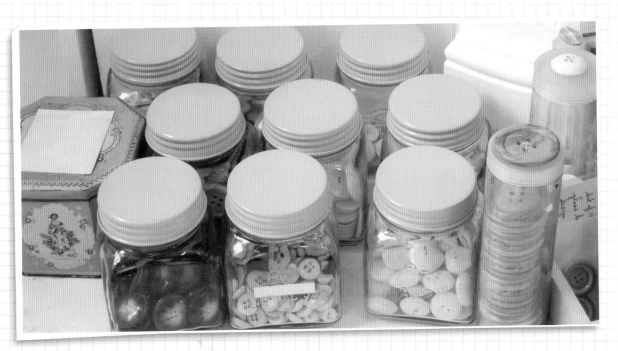

DIY toolkit

Don't rush out and buy everything at once. Look for good second hand items and car boot (trunk) sale finds. A complete toolkit builds over time.

Toolbox

Use something large and sturdy, with compartments. The best ones are strong enough to sit and even stand on.

Transparent containers

These are essential for quickly locating small things such as nails or screws and salvaged fixings from previous projects. Takeaway food containers are great.

Screws and nails

You only need a small starter selection. Build your collection as you tackle different projects.

Glues

Small containers of PVC glue, superglue, wood glue, all-purpose adhesive and epoxy resin will all come in handy.

Snub nose pliers

These come in various sizes – choose a pair that sits comfortably in your hand. The flat nose allows you to get a good grip when pulling nails out of wood.

Fine nose/pointed pliers

For more tricky manoeuvres and finer work such as closing links in jewellery making. There should be an inner cutting edge on all pliers for cutting or stripping wires.

Monkey wrench

This can be adjusted to fit a variety of nuts, bolts and pipes.

Clamps (various sizes)

To hold things steady, fix items to a work bench or hold surfaces together while glue sets.

Saw

A basic cross-cut saw for wood.

Hacksaw and blades

You will need these for more fiddly cutting jobs. Buy some replaceable blades for wood, and metal, as you may want to cut a pipe.

Hammer

Essential for driving nails.

Multi-head screwdriver

Find one with with both flat blades and crossheads of various sizes. A ratchet screwdriver takes a lot of the effort out of putting in and removing screws.

Heavy duty scissors

For DIY jobs around the house and garden.

Stanley/craft knife

The handle of these very sharp knives contains the blades when not in use.

Retractable tape measure

Also worth having a small steel ruler and a square for right angles.

Safety glasses

To wear when drilling.

Sandpaper and cork block

Have a stock of grades from coarse to fine sandpaper for different projects, from rubbing down walls to keying surfaces for repainting or varnishing. A wraparound cork block gives a good hold.

Power drill

Choose a good make with plenty of power and a range of bits to help you with a host of jobs.

Electric screwdriver

To avoid wrist ache if you do a lot of DIY.

Electric sander

If you do a lot of sanding it is worth having one of these with a variety of heads.

Joist, pipe and cable detector

Essential piece of safety kit to check before you drill through something.

SPRING

SPRING IS THE TIME FOR NEW GROWTH – BUT IT DOESN'T HAVE TO MEAN BUYING NEW THINGS. YOU CAN HAVE A NEW KITCHEN BY REVAMPING YOUR OLD CUPBOARDS, START GROWING VEGETABLES FROM SEED, EVEN MAKE YOUR OWN SPRING CLEANING MATERIALS.

Top tips for spring cleaning

These days we have become reliant on expensive cleaning chemicals, in the belief that they save us time and do a better job than the formulas our parents and grandparents used, but this is a myth!

It is really easy to make your own cleaning products that do just as good a job. They are cheaper and better for the environment, too.

YOU WILL NEED

These can be bought in supermarkets, hardware stores or pharmacies.

- White distilled vinegar (*acetic acid*)
- Baking soda (*sodium bicarbonate*)
- Borax (*sodium borate*) – a natural mineral compound that is excellent for a number of jobs around the home including stain and grease removal.
- Washing soda (*sodium carbonate*)
- Liquid soap (*sodium hydroxide*)
- Distilled water – you can use ordinary tap water, but distilled water is a better carrier and dirt solvent. Tap water often contains salts and minerals that can leave spotting and build-up.
- Essential oils – not only do they smell great, but they also have potent antibacterial effects. Try adding:

  Lemon – a clean, sweet, energizing deodorizer

  Peppermint – a fresh smell that is an air purifier and mild pest repellent

  Eucalyptus – a refreshing and therapeutic deodorizer

  Tea-tree – an anti-bacterial air and surface sanitizer

Recipes

For many spring cleaning chores, you can make your own cleaning products using the formulas listed below:

Basic cleaning fluid

500ml (18fl oz) water
½ teaspoon Borax
¼ teaspoon liquid soap
36 drops essential oil

Carpet cleaner

125g (4½oz) baking soda
1 teaspoon liquid soap
18 drops essential oil

Carpet freshener

125g (4½oz) baking soda
18 drops essential oil

Furniture polish

3 tablespoons vinegar
½ teaspoon jojoba oil
10 drops lemon essential oil

Gentle scouring cream

60g (6¾oz) baking soda
Liquid soap
18 drops essential oil
Add the essential oils to the baking soda and blend. Next, incorporate the liquid soap, several drops at a time, until a creamy paste forms.

Window cleaner

500ml (18fl oz) water
3 tablespoons vinegar
¼ teaspoon liquid soap
36 drops essential oil

Bottles

Before you start, make sure you have a good stock of basic spray bottles – you don't need to buy new bottles, just save the bottles from your existing cleaners and wash them out.

Kitchen cupboard makeovers

For an impressive transformation in your kitchen without the expense and upheaval of completely new units try painting the cupboards and making a feature of door panels and handles. Or use our instant dirt-busting cleaner to give them a new lease of life.

A coat of paint

Update cupboard doors with a new coat of paint for immediate glamour.

YOU WILL NEED

- Sugar soap
- Medium- to fine-grade sandpaper (or liquid deglosser)
- Undercoat
- Kitchen paint in chosen colours
- New handles (optional)

Prepare the surfaces

Make sure that the surfaces are free of grease by cleaning with sugar soap.

To 'key' the surface of the clean cupboard, cabinet or shelf, so that the new paint bonds to it, sand it down lightly but thoroughly with a medium- to fine-grade sandpaper.

Cupboards with a shiny finish will definitely need sanding before you can paint them. Alternatively, use a 'liquid deglosser' (also called liquid sander) available from DIY stores.

Paint with care

Remove the cupboard doors (and the hinges and handles). Carefully apply a thin coat of undercoat, followed by one or two thin top coats. Thin coats dry more easily and will give a smoother finish. Make sure each coat is dry before applying the next. Never be tempted to slap on a thick coat of paint hoping to cover the doors in one go!

Go for a specialist kitchen paint that is designed to withstand the heat, steam and repeated cleaning.

Add new handles

You could go for something ultra-modern or opt for a shabby chic look. We made some with old teaspoons.

To attach the teapoon, use a soldering iron, an epoxy adhesive or drill and screw to the door, depending on the structure and material of your door. A DIY beginner is better to stick to ready-made handles.

Tip

Unless there is a dreadful clash between the old colour and the new, you don't need to paint the backs of doors or the inside of the cupboards. Use masking tape so that the colour doesn't run over onto areas you don't want to paint.

Unusual finishes

Make a feature of door panels by using wallpaper and varnish or sticky back plastic, which comes in an array of designs.

To help keep your life organized, try painting one or two cupboard doors with black chalkboard paint. This is a great way to write reminders, shopping lists, to do lists, meal planners, appointments and more.

If you are feeling creative, a découpage finish is a fun and funky way to display favourite images. See our **Upcycled Chairs** project for full instructions.

The 'no paint' option

The problem with surfaces and walls is that they get covered in a greasy film. A quick wipe with a kitchen cloth only serves to move the grease about a bit. To give a new lease of life to old grimy cupboards without painting, try our homemade miracle kitchen cupboard cleaner.

YOU WILL NEED

For 1 bucket of cleaner:

- 125g (4½oz) Borax
- 10 drops essential oil
- 2 tablespoons washing-up liquid

Put all the ingredients in your bucket and fill with really hot water.

Use a soft sponge to wash down the cupboards, cabinets and shelves with the solution. Leave it to work for a couple of minutes, then wipe with a damp cloth that has also been dipped into the solution but rung almost dry.

Seriously greasy kitchens may need more than one application or more Borax in the solution.

New handles give a stylish finishing touch

Try blackboard paint or magnetic finishes

Mend It! Repairing clothes

Replacing zips

Just because a zip (zipper) is broken does not mean you have to throw your favourite trousers out.

Out with the old

Measure the existing zip and buy a new one the same type (nylon or metal), colour and length.

Remove the old zip using a seam ripper. Be careful not to tear the fabric. Once it is out you will be left with two pieces of material with creases where the zip was. Place the creases right-sides together and tack along the crease mark.

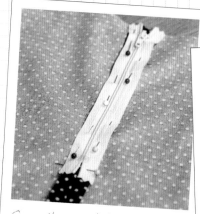

Secure the zip with dressmaking pins

A zip foot sews closely to the teeth

In with the new

With the zip face down, place the metal stopper that is at the base of the zip aligning the centre of the seam. Pin on each side to secure.

Fold the zip back and slowly 'walk' the zip up the seam, aligning the seam line with the centre of the teeth. Secure with dressmaking pins as you go. Sew the zip in place with loose tacking (basting) stitches.

When you are happy with the positioning, sew it firmly in place by hand, or ideally with a sewing machine so the stitching is more secure. Remove all tacking stitches and finish off raw edges.

By machine

On the right side of the fabric, starting on one side of the zip at the top, with the zip foot on your sewing machine set to the outside position, sew down towards the end of the zip.

Stop, leave the needle in the fabric and lift the presser foot to turn the fabric around.

Lower the foot and continue sewing across the end of the zip, turning the fabric again to go back up the other side. Finish off and unpick your tacking stitches.

Tips

- When sewing the zip (zipper) in place, keep a constant distance from the centre of the zip. If you stitch too close to the mechanism it won't run cleanly.
- If a metal zip is a bit sticky, rub a pencil over the teeth. The graphite acts as a lubricant. For a plastic zip, use soap.

Fixing or altering hems

If you can hem, you can shorten skirts and trousers, alter tops and dresses and refashion lots of your clothes.

YOU WILL NEED

- Seam ripper
- Iron
- Ironing board
- Dressmaking pins
- Fabric chalk
- Scissors
- Sewing needle
- Thread

Preparation

Using a seam ripper, carefully unpick the hem of the skirt. Press the original hemline out of the fabric with an iron.

Put the garment on. Decide how long you want it and mark the new length with pins. (Get a friend to help you with this step.)

Place tape on the inside of the hem

Press the tape into place

If necessary, cut away any excess fabric leaving about 5cm (2in) to fold up and create a neat hem.

Turn in a fold of about 1cm (⅜in) along the bottom of the fabric and press. Bring the folded edge of the fabric up to the desired new length and press the hem into place. Secure with pins.

Stitch the hem by hand with a blind stitch to ensure the sewing thread doesn't show on the right side of the garment. Or use a standard stitch on a machine to give a visible hem.

Hemming without sewing

If you are in a hurry or don't want to sew, use an iron-on hemming tape – a gauzy material that comes on a roll or card.

Measure hem as above. After you have pressed the hem in place, insert the tape into the folded portion of the hem. Use an iron to seal the hem, placing a damp cloth between the fabric and the iron to prevent scorching.

Use a blind stitch for an invisible hem

Tip

If you want to remove iron-on hemming tape, place a damp cloth over the area and apply an iron, then peel the layers apart.

'Open Sesame' door stop

Fix that annoying door that is always drifting shut, with a handmade door stop. It is a quick and easy thing to make and is filled with uncooked rice, sand or dried beans. You can make it to coordinate with the fabrics in your room or use a bright funky fabric to make it a feature.

YOU WILL NEED

- 35cm (14in) of cotton fabric
- 35cm (14in) of iron-on interlining
- Small piece of contrasting fabric or ribbon
- Dressmaking pins
- Matching thread
- Uncooked rice, sand or dried beans to fill

Cut out the fabric

Cut out the following pieces:

- 1 square 18 x 18cm (7 x 7in) from main fabric
- 4 triangles – with base of 16cm (6¼in) and height of 16cm (6¼in) from main fabric
- 1 square 18 x 18cm (7 x 7in) from interlining
- 4 triangles – with base of 16cm (6¼in) and height of 16cm (6¼in) from interlining
- A strip 16 x 8cm (6¼ x 3⅛in) in the contrasting fabric

Fuse the interlining to the fabric

Place the interlining, glue side down, onto the wrong side of each fabric piece and iron it to the fabric.

Make the carry handle

Take the strip of contrasting fabric and folding it with rights sides together, sew a 1cm (⅜in) seam along the long side. Turn the tube right side out. Fold the fabric so that the seam runs along the middle and press with an iron. Put on one side.

Sew the panels together and attach the handle

With right sides together, machine stitch two of the fabric triangles together along one of the long sides. Press open the seam. Repeat with the remaining two fabric triangles. Place the stitched triangle pairs on top of each other, matching the raw edges.

Take the carry handle and fold it in half so that the seam is now inside the fold. Place the open ends in the middle of the triangle peaks between the two layers of fabric.

Leaving a small opening on one of the long sides, pin and then machine stitch the remaining long sides together to create a pyramid, with the handle coming out of the top.

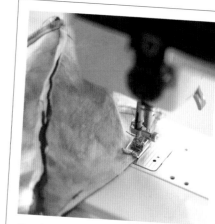

Machine stitch the triangles together

Place the handle between the two layers

Press the seams open. Clip across the seam allowance at the apex of the triangle to neaten.

Sew the pyramid to the base with the **right sides together**, pin the square base to the bottom edges of the pyramid and machine in place, one side at a time, pivoting at the corners. Trim the seams at the corners. Turn the pyramid right side out.

Fill the pyramid and finish off
Using a kitchen funnel inserted into the gap you have left in the side seam, fill your pyramid with rice, sand or beans. Put the narrow end of the cone into the gap and pour in the rice or other filling. Slip stitch the opening closed.

Scotty Dog Doorstop
For a cute variation on the same theme.

YOU WILL NEED
- 50cm (20in) of cotton fabric
- Dog template (see **Templates** section)
- Dressmaking pins
- Needle and cotton
- Polyester wadding (batting) for filling
- Dried pulses to fill
- Old buttons for eyes and noses
- Ribbon to decorate

Cut out the fabric
Cut out the fabric pieces using the templates.

Make the dog
Attach the gusset to the head. With right sides facing, match up and pin the ears (point **A**) of gusset to the ears on the head, nose (point **B**) to nose and back of head (point **C**) and pin. Stitch together.

Stitch together both sides of the underbelly, but leave a gap of about 5cm (2in) to allow you to insert the filling later.

Match up and pin points **D** and **E** of the underbelly to the main body. Stitch together.

Match up both sides of the main body and stitch together, leaving the feet open.

Pin and attach the feet gussets to the feet – this will give you a firm base for your doorstop to stand on.

Fill the doorstop
Turn right side out and stuff. Start filling by inserting the polyester wadding (batting) into the ears, head and tail. Continue to fill until about half full. This wadding will help the dog to retain its shape. Fill the remainder of the body and the feet with the dried pulses. Slip stitch the opening closed.

To finish, sew on buttons for the eyes and a nose. Tie a pretty bow round the dog's neck.

Note: If you only use dried pulses all the filling will fall to the bottom and the doorstop will lose its shape.

Tip
You don't need to spend a lot for projects like this. The little grey dog was made from an old sweatshirt, the eyes and noses were spare buttons and the ribbons saved from gift wraps.

Recycling in the garden

There is nothing more satisfying than growing plants from seed and seeing the first little green shoots burst through the compost. It is also cheaper than buying small plants. No need to buy plant pots for your garden seedlings either! Make your own using toilet roll tubes or old newspapers.

Toilet roll pots

Take a toilet roll tube and make four slits around one end of the tube to create four flaps. Each flap should be about 5cm (2in) in length. Fold in the four little flaps like a box bottom and stand upright on a tray.

Fill the pots with potting compost. Press the compost down firmly with your fingers.

Sow your seeds. Remember to keep the pots well watered!

When the seedlings are ready, there is no need to transplant them and disturb their roots. Just plant the whole pots out in the ground where the cardboard will eventually rot away.

Or, use old newspaper to make little pots. Just fold a sheet of paper slightly longer than the required length, roll into a tube shape and push one end in. Fill with compost and plant your seeds.

Cloches from plastic bottles

Don't worry about late frosts – use empty plastic bottles to make mini cloches. Cut the bottom off and place the bottle over the pot.

We prettied these up by painting the screw caps and making some little salt dough plant identifier tags (see our **Salt Dough** recipe) tied on with string.

Tip

Hold onto your plastic bottles, they are really useful for all sorts of things in the garden. If you stick them in the ground the other way up and secure them with plant canes, they funnel water directly to a plant's roots.

Make sourdough bread

Making sourdough bread is one of the most satisfying baking experiences. It is real slow food and the slower you make it, the better the flavour and texture of your loaves. Sourdough bread is made without added yeast. It begins with a 'starter' – the fermentation that cultivates the wild, naturally occurring yeasts that make bread rise.

Making a sourdough starter

A starter is a living thing and once created, needs a little nurturing and feeding to keep it alive. If looked after properly, it can last for years. In the early days, it is a hungry beast and needs feeding twice daily until it is a fully fermented organic mass.

YOU WILL NEED

- 500g (1lb 2oz) unbleached strong white bread flour (organic if possible)
- 1 litre (1¾ pints) water
- Small bunch organic red grapes
- Piece of muslin (cheesecloth)

Note: There is no added yeast, no sugar and definitely no salt. Salt slows down the fermentation and the good bacteria at the root of all good sourdough.

Bringing the ingredients together

Whisk the flour and water in a large non-metallic bowl to a smooth batter. Wash the grapes and tie them in a muslin cloth. Lightly crush them – to break the skins – then immerse the bag in the batter. The grapes provide natural yeast that covers their skins.

Use a plate to cover the bowl and put it in a safe place at room temperature for 10 days.

Ready to feed

After 10 days, the bag will be puffy with escaping gas; there will be a distinctive 'ripe' smell about the batter and it will have a pink tinge from the grapes. Lift out the bag, squeeze out any juice and discard the grapes. Stir, then throw away 250g (9oz) of the mixture, so there is room to add new ingredients to 'feed' the starter.

Let the feeding commence

Feed the starter **twice a day for two weeks** until it is ready to make bread. For each feed you need:

- 100g (3½oz) unbleached strong white bread flour (organic if possible)
- 150ml (¼ pint) water

Make a batter with the new flour and water and stir into the starter. Cover and leave at room temperature for 12 hours. Discard 250g (9oz) of the batter and add another batch of new batter feed. Carry on this 'feeding' routine every day for two weeks. The starter will become increasingly active with more bubbles.

Throwing away this amount of batter each time seems wasteful, but it is essential, otherwise the starter would take over your entire home!

Ready to bake

After two weeks of twice daily feeding, the mix will be visibly very lively. It should have a slight fizz to it when you taste a bit. If not, continue feeding for a couple more days. The surface will be covered with bubbles. It is now home to billions of helpful microbes! You need 250g (9oz) of the starter for your first batch of bread.

Taking care of your starter

Whenever you use some starter, replace what you have used with 100g (3½oz) flour mixed with 150ml (¼ pint) water, added to the rest of the starter. Mix thoroughly. Keep it in the refrigerator in a screw-top jar.

If you don't make any bread for a couple of weeks, take out 250g (9oz) of the starter and feed the remainder with new flour and water.

Baking sourdough bread

The following recipe is for a white loaf made with a white flour-based starter. It makes 3 x 450g (1lb) loaf tins or 2 x 900g (2lb) tins.

YOU WILL NEED

- 250g (9oz) sourdough starter
- 800–900g (1¾–2lb) unbleached strong white bread flour (organic if possible), plus extra for dusting
- 450ml (¾ pint) cold water
- 10–15g (¼–½oz) sea salt
- olive oil, for greasing

Timing

It is impossible to give fixed timings for this recipe, as many factors can change the action of the bacterium; temperature, type of flour, time since the starter's last feed or how long it has been out of the refrigerator.

You can start as much as 48 hours ahead if you want. The important thing is to allow your uncooked loaves about 5 hours to rise – sometimes it can take 24 hours.

16–24 hours ahead

Take the sourdough starter and mix thoroughly with the cold water and 400g (14oz) of the flour. A large wire whisk is perfect. Cover with a cloth and leave overnight in a coolish place – for 16 hours, but ideally more – to allow the natural yeasts to react. This creates the 'sponge' and is the base of your bread.

16–24 hours later

The starter will have been vigorously feeding off the flour and water. It will smell fresh and 'yeasty' and be very bubbly.

Gradually add another 400–500g (14oz–1lb 2oz) flour to the dough – possibly more, it is about getting the right consistency. Beat in the flour and beat out the lumps. It will take about 10 minutes by hand, or use a mixer with a bread hook for 5 minutes.

Add the salt. Sourdough needs more salt than yeast-based bread to balance the sourness of the dough. Taste the dough at this stage.

Kneading the dough

Turn the sticky dough out onto a clean worktop – don't flour it or add any more flour to the dough. As you knead it, it will become a lot less sticky. Knead for about 5 minutes by continually stretching and folding and throwing onto the worktop so it gets progressively stiffer and silkier, though it won't get as 'unsticky' as yeast-based dough.

Sourdough is only handled once this way and there is no 'knocking-back'. When it is smooth and stickily silky, it is ready to shape.

Tip

The cooler the place you make and store your dough, the longer the fermentation process and the better the flavour and texture of the bread.

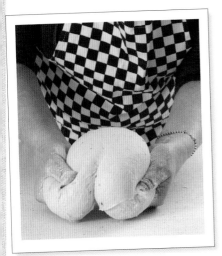

Shaping the loaves

Oil the bread tins well with a pastry brush, including the top rim as the dough can rise up and stick to the rim and is very hard to remove. Dust the tins with flour.

Split the dough into even parts and place into the tins. It should fill no more than half the tin. Leave in a cool place for 3–5 hours to rise. When the dough has reached the top of the tin, it is ready to bake.

Baking

Pre-heat the oven to 230°C/450°F/Gas Mark 8. Place a small tray of cold water at the bottom of the oven to create steam and form a better crust.

Bake for 15 minutes, then reduce heat to 200°C/400°F/Gas Mark 6 and bake for a further 15 minutes. Don't open the oven door.

Remove from the oven and knock the loaves out of the tins. Tap the base of each with your knuckles or a wooden spoon; if they sound hollow they are done.

Place them back into the oven for 3–5 minutes to fully crisp the crust. Leave to cool on a wire rack.

Tip

Silicon-coated baking tin liners are very useful as no oil is needed.

The dough should fill no more than half the tin

SUMMER

WHAT'S NICER THAN PUTTING YOUR FEET UP IN THE SUMMER AND SITTING OUT IN THE SUNSHINE? YOU CAN LAZE ABOUT IN STYLE ON OUR HANDMADE CUSHIONS, WHILE YOUR FRIENDS ENJOY FOOD COOKED ON YOUR HOME-MADE BARBECUE.

Upcycled garden planter

Here is an example of re-using something that has passed its usefulness. Often we assume if something is old and not needed it has to be sent to the dump. A little imagination can give old rubbish a new purpose and a new home – in this case, out of the fireplace and into the garden! Here is how we upcycled a grate basket into a garden container.

YOU WILL NEED
- Empty fire grate basket
- Felt hanging basket liner – about 50cm (19in)
- A bag of general purpose compost
- Herb plants or seedlings

Prepare the liner
Cut a piece of felt liner to fit the grate basket. Lay the liner over the grate, pushing it into the corners, and cut round the edges. Cut it slightly bigger than the grate, as it will drop down when you add the compost.

Fill and plant
Fill the planter with general purpose compost and trim back any excess felt round the edges.
  Plant your herbs and water well. Don't let the container dry out.

Suggested herbs
Try a mixture of sage, thyme and dill, plus nasturtiums to give some colour and to trail over the edges.

Don't let the container dry out

Tip
If the container is shallow, keep it well watered. Add some water retaining crystals to the compost to cut down on watering frequency.

Top tips to revamp your holiday wardrobe

The beach is waiting and you have nothing to wear? What about that overstuffed wardrobe and those boxes of unwanted clothes in the spare room? Here is how to revamp last year's summer clothes and look absolutely fabulous darling.

1. Sort out your wardrobe

Ask yourself:
- Does it fit?
- Do I truly like it?
- Does the colour flatter me?
- Does it make me feel really good?

Anything that doesn't tick any of the boxes should be put in a separate pile to go through later and decide if they can be altered to fit or made over for a new lease of life – see Tip 5.

2. Refresh your whites

Keep your summer whites, white!
Soak items for a couple of hours in a mixture of hot water and lemon slices or white vinegar. After washing in the normal way, hang on the line – sunlight is nature's greatest bleach.

3. Decide on a colour palette and stick to it

Buying lots of random clothes might cheer you up in the short term, but it won't give you lots of outfits to wear. If you limit your palette to a few colours that blend and tone you will have more choice.

4. Accent with colour

If you want to wear this season's colours, invest in a few accent pieces that enhance your outfit such as cheap T-shirts.

5. Adapt and update

Before you throw something away, think about whether you can modernize it or revamp it. Clothes that are now boring can be made into a brand new outfit. Think of shortening trousers into Capri pants or shorts, dresses becoming skirts, cutting sleeves off tops, or restyling necklines.

6. Get creative

Use magazines for inspiration and try mixing and matching your pieces to see how they can be worn in new ways. You will be amazed at how many new outfits you can create just by layering, clashing colours and combining smart with casual clothes.

7. Accessorize

Good accessories can change an outfit from glum to glam in a matter of moments. Beg, borrow or steal bags, scarves, sunglasses, jewellery and shoes – flip-flops and cheap sandals can be stylish and fun, and a great way of refreshing an outfit.

8. Have a clothes swap party

Gather your friends together to swap clothes, footwear and accessories for free. It is a great way of recycling your unwanted clothes and bagging yourself a real bargain. One woman's cast offs are another girl's steal.

9. Shop for what you need, not what you want

Think carefully before you buy and only invest in items that can multitask from day to night, or casual to dressy. Don't obsess over the latest must-haves, focus on what you need to finish off your look. Do you really need another pair of shoes? Perhaps not, but maybe a statement necklace could be just the thing to bring your little black dress or classic white shirt bang on trend.

10. Swimwear

One thing worth investing in is a really good swimsuit or bikini, especially if you are on the curvaceous side. If you are feeling creative you could try making your own. A simple basic bikini is easy to make and can look fabulous if you make it in an unusual fabric.

Make your own barbecue

Some of the barbecues on offer are as big as an Aga and as flashy as a spaceship – but do they work that well? How much space do they take up? Do you have to buy elaborate covers for them? Do you have to put them in the garage in the winter? And more importantly, are you sacrificing that authentic, charcoal roasted flavour for commercial convenience?

A brick barbecue

This simple brick hexagonal barbecue stays out in all weathers without rusting and it is tall enough that you don't have to stoop. It looks good, cooks food with a great flavour, and best of all you can make it very cheaply using leftover house bricks.

YOU WILL NEED

- About 90 house bricks (as many layers of 6 bricks as you wish)
- Circular piece of heatproof metal about 6mm (¼in) thick, with several holes drilled in. It needs to be a size that will sit neatly on top of the hexagon.
- Circular metal grill for cooking

Build the base

Arrange six bricks in a hexagon shape in the area you have chosen as your permanent barbecue site. This should be firm, level ground or concrete hard standing.

Build up the layers, arranging the bricks in an offset hexagon arrangement. Continue until you have 11 or 12 layers.

Insert the fuel tray

You need a circular piece of heatproof metal with several holes drilled in it for the air to circulate. This acts as your fire base for charcoal or wood and the holes in it allow air to be drawn up from underneath and from the gaps in the bricks below. You can get one made to your dimensions at a local forge or builder's yard.

Build up the last 3 or 4 layers

A total of 14 layers (84 bricks) seems to suit both men and women but you can go for 13 layers (78 bricks) or 15 (90 bricks), depending on your height and comfort.

Recycle a grill from an old barbecue

To cook your food, use any grill that fits – you can use one from an old barbecue. If the fire gets too hot, just add another course of 6 bricks to raise the height of the griddle. It is a good idea to keep 6 bricks handy on the ground just in case you want a gentler, slower cook.

Any ashes from the fire just fall within itself into the space below or can be swept up from the circular fuel tray if the holes block up.

Bucket barbecue

You can make a barbecue from virtually anything. Disposable ones are just tinfoil trays with a bit of charcoal inside and some wire mesh over the top. Why pay a fortune for those only to have to chuck them away? Just buy a bag of charcoal and use your ingenuity.

A home-made portable barbie is great for taking away camping or for a day out. They are also useful if you live in an apartment with a balcony or have a very small garden and little space.

YOU WILL NEED

- Galvanised bucket (an old leaky one will do) or a biscuit tin, an old cake tin or any metal container
- Hammer and a large diameter nail
- 5 metal rods (heat resistant) or some sturdy wire

Make the holes

Use the nail to hammer holes around the diameter of the container, about 5cm (2in) apart.

About 5cm (2in) above the holes hammer in another 5 holes on one side of the bucket about 2.5–3.5cm (1–1½in) apart and the same number of holes directly opposite on the other side of the bucket.

This second set of holes needs to be spaced so that when you thread through the metal rods or wire your charcoal fuel doesn't fall between them. So mark your bucket up first. Depending on its size you may need more rods.

Make the grill

Having marked up your container, measure the distance between the 5 holes on either side and add another 5cm (2in). This gives you the length of your rods, so do this before you buy them.

Thread the metal rods through the 5 holes on one side of your bucket and out of the 5 holes opposite. Then bend the ends so they stay in place. Lay the charcoal on top of the rods. If you are using wire, follow the method as for the rods but make more holes so you can criss-cross the wires to make a bed for the charcoal.

To cook, either put your food on skewers wider than the diameter of the bucket, or salvage a metal rack that you can rest on top of the bucket – one from an old grill pan will do perfectly.

Pile them high cushions

Adding new cushions to a piece of furniture can really lift a room and make it seem like new, but they can cost a fortune. This need not be the case. With minimal outlay and a little time and effort you can have fabulous new cushions that not only look great, but are real originals.

Simple cushion cover

Anyone, even a complete novice can make this basic, easy cushion cover.

YOU WILL NEED

• Cushion pad
• Enough fabric to cover the pad
• Dressmaking pins
• Matching thread

Choosing your fabric

If you are new to sewing, a cotton fabric is easiest to work with. Otherwise you can find fabric anywhere – in remnant baskets at the shops, old curtains, clothes and jumpers. In fact, any scraps you can get your hands on.

Cutting out

Measure the cushion pad, length and width. Beginners may want to make a pattern first. To do this, simply mark out the measurements of the cushion pad on a piece of paper and add another 3cm (1¼in) to each length as seam allowance.

Fold the fabric in half. Secure the pattern to the fabric with pins and cut out to make two identical pieces.

Sewing up the cover

Remove the pattern and place the two fabric pieces right sides together and pin. Stitch them together by machining down three sides of the fabric pieces, leaving one side open.

Finishing off

Turn the cover inside out, so the right side is outermost, press and insert the cushion pad. Fold in the remaining open edges and stitch the open seam together.

   You now have a new cushion at a fraction of the price of a shop bought one.

Tip

If you want a zipped cushion put in your zip (zipper) first – see **Mend it! Repairing Clothes** – and then sew up the three sides. But don't forget to unzip before you sew up the last side!

Designer cushion cover

Get the designer look by using fabric scraps to make a cushion cover that look a million dollars. Use remnants, old clothes… even tea towels or shirts. It is what you do with the fabric that counts.

YOU WILL NEED

- A mixture of fabric scraps and remnants
- Cushion pad
- Matching thread
- Zip (zipper) (optional)

Preparation

Make a template for your cover – the size of your cushion pad plus 3–4cm (1¼–1½in) all round for your seams.

Sort the fabric. Have a play around to see which fabrics go well together. You want a good blend of colours and pieces that will fit the pad size once they are sewn together.

Making the cover pieces

Once you are happy with your design, cut the fabric pieces to size, remembering to include seam allowances. Stitch them together to make the front cover.

You can repeat this process for the back of your cover or use a plain piece of fabric as we have done here.

Insert a zip if required

Chose whether you are going to use a zip (zipper) fastener or simply hand stitch the open side closed. If you are putting in a zip follow the instructions in **Mend it! Repairing Clothes**.

Sew up

Stitch the two halves of the cushion cover together, making sure you only stitch along three sides and leave one side open (unless it is the zipped side – in which case leave the zip undone so you can turn the cushion the right way out).

Insert the cushion pad and finish off

Turn the cushion cover right side out and insert the pad.

Hand stitch the fourth side closed (unless you have added a zip) by folding the raw edges over, tucking them inside and sewing together.

And that's it. Dress up your sofa and sit back and admire.

Have a play around to see which fabrics go together

Vintage cake stand

Traditional afternoon tea is back! Victorian-style cake stands are bang on trend, but come with a hefty price tag. This little stunner is really cheap and easy to make.

YOU WILL NEED

- 3 plates
- Cutting board
- Masking tape
- Tape measure
- Felt-tip pen
- Supports – you can buy these cheaply online. Search for 'cake stand supports'.
- 5mm (³⁄₁₆in) ceramic drill bit
- Electric drill
- White spirit

Fix the support fitting to the plate

Tip

Use a special 5mm (³⁄₁₆in) ceramic/tile bit in a power drill on a slow speed to avoid shattering the plates.

Select your plates

Find three plates. Root around car boot (trunk) sales, garage sales or charity (thrift) shops for cheap ones. Go for plates of varying sizes, colours or patterns that look good together.

Prepare your work surface

Use a proper cutting board so you don't drill through the work surface.

It is a good idea to use a stand to hold the plate in place while you are drilling. A roll of masking tape works perfectly.

Find the centre of your plates

Take a small strip of masking tape and stick it in the middle of the plate. Get a tape measure and mark the centre with a dot of felt-tip pen.

Drill the hole

The most important thing to remember when drilling plates is to be gentle. Use a light touch and a slow speed. Porcelain plates take longer and can get very hot, so handle with care. When drilling porcelain it is a good idea to have some lubricant to hand, such as white spirit to keep the drill tip and the plate cool.

Attach the support fitting

Attach a plastic washer to the thread and fix to the plate. Put another washer above and connect to the next piece of fitting. Shop-bought fittings come with plastic washers.

Fill with cakes, sit back and relax with a cup of tea!

Mend It! Upcycling

Do you ever look at a piece of well loved furniture and think it has seen better days? Or thought that it doesn't fit with the look of your room? And do you think about chucking it away? Really? Stop.

Rather than take it to the dump, why not have a go at upcycling it into something you will love again? Look at renovating and refurbishing old dining chairs for instance. It is amazing what you can do with a little elbow grease, a few tacks and a lot of inspiration.

Painting and re-upholstering

It is easy to breath life into your old chairs with a simple paint job and new seat cover.

YOU WILL NEED

- Old wooden dining chair
- Fine-grade sandpaper
- Oil based paint – either gloss or satin finish (eggshell) – or varnish
- Paintbrush
- Webbing strips
- Upholstery fabric (It is best to use upholstery weight fabric as it is harder wearing.)
- Hammer
- Tacks
- Staple gun

Gently sand the chair

Replace the seat padding if worn

Preparing and painting your chair

Pop out the seat base. It may need a little pressure. Put this to one side to repair and re-cover later.

Clean the chair with soapy water, removing dust and dirt from the corners. Gently sand with fine-grade sandpaper or an electric sander. You don't need to remove all the paint completely. Just remove the loose paint or varnish to create a smooth surface for painting. Wipe the dust away with a damp rag.

Apply a thin coat of paint or varnish. Let it dry thoroughly and give it a light rub down with a very fine-grade sandpaper, then repeat the process. Leave it to dry.

Repairing the seat base

If the chair is sagging, fix the webbing strips underneath by removing the top layers and tightening up the webbing or replacing it with new strips. Replace the padding if necessary and then re-cover.

Re-covering the seat

To re-cover the seat pad, remove the top layer of fabric. Using this as a template, lay it on top of the new fabric and cut around it. Leave enough fabric to fold underneath the chair.

Place the seat pad face down on the wrong side of the fabric and pull it taut. Hammer one side secure with

Use the old fabric cover as your template

Staple while stretching the fabric

tacks or a staple gun. Repeat on the opposite side, and continue tacking or stapling all the way around, while stretching the cover taut.

Once the chair is thoroughly dry, put the restored seat pad back in.

Découpage a chair

Découpage is a French term meaning to 'cut up'. This eighteenth-century craft form is enjoying a renaissance and is an inexpensive way to breathe life into old furniture.

YOU WILL NEED

- Old wooden chair
- Old magazines, books, newspapers or images – we used comics
- Craft knife
- Cutting mat
- Metal ruler
- Small scissors
- Glue – PVA (white) glue or mod podge
- Lint-free cloth
- Small paintbrush
- Large paintbrush
- Matt varnish
- Fine-grade sandpaper

Preparing your chair

Prepare the chair as in the first project – you don't need a perfect finish as you will be covering the wood up.

Preparing your images

Use images from old magazines, books, posters, sheet music or newspapers. With a craft knife and metal ruler, cut the images out. We started with square/oblong shapes to build up the background, then added more detailed images later. Use a cutting mat so you don't scratch your work surface.

Applying the images

Experiment with the layout before gluing. Cover the whole surface with images that fit together, or overlap them and build up the layers by placing smaller shapes over larger ones.

Take an image, apply glue to the back then stick it onto the chair. Pat with your finger, then smooth with a clean lint-free cloth to remove any bubbles. Make sure the edges are well stuck. Apply more glue if you need to.

Continue this process until you have completely covered your chair.

Apply a coat of clear, matt varnish

Finishing off

Apply a coat of clear, matt varnish with a medium brush over the whole chair. Leave it to dry overnight. When the varnish is completely dry, apply up to 10 more coats at intervals. Wait for each coat to dry completely. Sand over your design lightly and wipe the dust away. Alternate the direction of the brushstrokes between each layer.

That's it! A brand new, unique piece of furniture, upcycled from something that could have ended up in the dump.

Use a sharp craft knife to cut out images

Hang out the bunting

There is nothing nicer on a warm summer's day than inviting friends and family round, and some brightly coloured bunting will give a real touch of style to your garden party or barbecue. This project is easy-peasy to do and can be made from any old leftover fabric.

YOU WILL NEED

- Fabric – a selection of leftover scraps will do
- Pinking shears
- 5m (197in) of tape – bias binding is perfect
- Dressmaking pins
- Needle and thread

Cut out your triangles

Using the pinking shears, cut out lots of triangles – approximately 12 x 15cm (4¾ x 6in). You don't have to use pinking shears, but if you don't, you will need to hem the edges of the triangles to stop them from fraying.

Work out the sequence

Lay the triangles on the floor and work out the best order of colours and patterns.

Once you are happy with the order, lay out the tape on a hard surface and place the triangles on top – about half way up the width of the tape.

Attach the tape to the triangles

Fold the tape over the edge of the triangles and pin in place. Make sure that you trap the triangle within the tape.

Stitch the triangles to the tape. This can be done by machine or by hand. Hang your bunting out in the garden and have a celebratory glass of wine!

Have fun with the order of colours and patterns

Tip

Any fabric – clothes, old sheets, tablecloths, tea towels – will do, as long as you intersperse plainer pieces with bolder colours and prints.

AUTUMN

'SEASON OF MISTS AND MELLOW FRUITFULNESS' – THE PERFECT TIME TO MAKE JAMS AND PRESERVES AND BOTTLE YOUR OWN SLOE GIN. SO GET YOUR HANDMADE APRON ON AND GET IN THE KITCHEN. AND AS THE NIGHTS DRAW IN SNUGGLE UP UNDER A QUILT MADE FROM OLD SWEATSHIRTS – VERY COSY.

Top tips for jam making and preserving

Making jam, conserves, marmalades, chutneys and pickles is not a dark art. There is a kind of mystery around preserving that stops many people having a go, but the satisfaction when you have potted up a batch of blackberry jam, strawberry conserve or green tomato chutney is fantastic.

1. Fruit and vegetable quality

Use good quality fresh fruit and vegetables to give flavour, texture and appearance. Don't use over-ripe and rotting fruits. Cut out the bad bits if you are making jam or chutney, but for whole vegetables or fruits like green tomatoes in oil or pickled cherries, they must look good as well as taste delicious.

2. Sterilization

Make sure your tools and equipment are extremely clean. Wash jars thoroughly, then sterilize by heating in a 110°C/225°F/Gas Mark ¼ oven for

about 15 minutes, just before filling. If you are using screw-top lids, either buy new or make sure old ones are really clean and not rusty. Boil the lids immediately before using. They need to be totally dry before sealing the jars or use cellophane covers.

3. Sugar – more than sweetness

Sugar is the main preserving ingredient and one of the keys to a good set. Before boiling the jam, all the sugar must be fully dissolved, or your jam won't set and can crystallize. Warm the sugar in the oven for 10 minutes before adding to the pan to help it dissolve.

Bring soft fruit to a gentle boil to release all their juice before adding the warm sugar. With firmer fruit, such as cherries or peaches, make sure the fruit has really softened before adding the sugar.

4. Setting jam

You don't need a thermometer to get a good set. Before starting, put three small plates in the freezer. Once your jam is at a rolling boil, test after 3 minutes. Drop a small blob on a frozen plate and tip it. The jam should run but will immediately cool so you can push on it with your finger. If it wrinkles like a skin, it is ready. If not, carry on boiling and test again every minute.

How set is another question. The longer you boil, the firmer the set. For the glossiest, most jewel-like appearance, you want 'just set'.

5. Pectin or no pectin (or lemon)

The amount of pectin in fruit varies. With low- and medium-pectin fruits, add lemon juice, or commercial pectin (in the sugar section of the supermarket). Jam sugar already contains pectin. With high-pectin, and most medium-pectin, fruits you don't need to add more.
- High-pectin – redcurrants, blackcurrants, damsons, quinces, apples and gooseberries.
- Medium-pectin – early blackberries, apricots, raspberries and loganberries.
- Low-pectin – strawberries, late blackberries, cherries, pears and elderberries.

6. Handling scum

All boiled preserves produce scum. It is just a sugary foam and not bad in any way, but you don't want it in your jars. Right at the end, add 10g (¼oz) of butter to disperse it and skim off the rest, once the pan is off the heat.

7. Help! – it has gone wrong

There is usually a remedy. The only thing that can really ruin your jam is burning the bottom. It leaves a bad taste, so keep a hawk eye and a moving spoon to stop things sticking on the bottom.
- Won't set? Tip it all back in the pan, add a bit more pectin or lemon juice, bring to the boil and test again.
- Over-boiled? Spread out on an oiled tray or silicon liner, dry and turn into fruit leather. Use in kids' lunch-boxes – not an E number in sight.
- Too stiff? So what… call it a marmalade. It will still taste absolutely delicious.

8. Setting chutney

Chutney takes far longer than jam – you are boiling away vinegar and melding far more ingredients. Look for the moment when you pull your spoon along the bottom of the pan and a clear channel opens, exposing the bottom of the pan like the parting of the Red Sea, before closing over again.

9. Hot preserve in hot pots

Pouring preserves into jars is a bit hazardous. Use a jam funnel – a wide topped, low funnel – to avoid spillages and safely transfer boiling jam from the pan with a ladle.

Label your jars

Most jams, pickles and chutneys will keep for at least six months sealed up. But it helps to know what is in the jar and when it was made. Don't even think of labelling your jars until they are quite cold!

If you are giving preserves as gifts, why not design a special label? This is really easy with a computer and printer. Then, maybe make some pretty cloth lid covers from remnant fabric and a bit of ribbon.

Courgette relish

Courgettes (zucchini) are abundant in autumn, and if you grow your own can leave you with a glut of fruit. There is nothing worse than food going to waste because you have so much that you don't know what to do with it. This delicious recipe is a simple treat to make and keeps for up to six months.

YOU WILL NEED

- 1kg (2¼ lb) courgettes (zucchini), finely grated
- 2 large onions, grated
- 2 red (bell) peppers, finely sliced
- 75g (2¾oz) salt
- 500ml (18fl oz) white wine vinegar
- 500ml (18fl oz) cider vinegar
- 2 tablespoons turmeric powder
- 300g (10½oz) caster (superfine) sugar
- 1 tablespoon English mustard powder
- 1 tablespoon cornflour (cornstarch)
- 1 tablespoon black peppercorns
- Finely chopped leaves from 1 celery head or 1 heaped tablespoon celery salt

EQUIPMENT

- 1 large bowl (glass, ceramic or stainless steel)
- 1 stainless steel pan (not aluminium or copper)
- Jam funnel
- 6–8 smallish sterilized jars (works best in small quantities)

Salting

Adding salt extracts excess water from the vegetables, intensifying their flavour.

Grate the courgettes (zucchini) and onions and finely slice the red (bell) peppers. Use the disc attachments on your food processor if you have one. Sprinkle with salt, mix well and cover. Leave overnight.

The next day, thoroughly rinse the vegetables to get rid of the salt – drain and squeeze out all remaining liquid using a clean tea towel. If they are still a bit wet, boil for a bit longer.

Boiling

Put the vegetables and all the other ingredients into a stainless steel pan and bring to the boil, stirring until all the sugar has dissolved. Simmer gently for about 20 minutes, stirring occasionally to prevent sticking. When the chutney has thickened to a slightly sludgy texture and there is not very much obvious liquid left – it is ready.

Jar and seal

Pot up into sterilized jars using a jam funnel. Cool completely before sealing. Label and store… but you will find yourself diving straightinto a jar! Once opened eat within a week.

Wonderful served with cheese, perfect with ham, delicious mixed with mayonnaise into a zingy dressing for a salad.

Make an apron in an hour

Sewing your own apron is a must for any modern maker-and-mender. If you are a beginner this project is a cinch to do and makes a great gift.

YOU WILL NEED

- About 1m (39¼in) of fabric
- Scissors
- Dressmaking pins
- Sewing machine and thread
- Matching or contrasting ribbon for ties – allow 2m (78¾in)
- Pinking shears

Choose your fabric

Recycle a duvet cover or a tablecloth or, if it is a gift, have a rummage in the remnant section at your fabric store. You can often get beautiful fabric for next to nothing.

Prepare a template

Find an apron the right size and lay it on top of your fabric. Pin it in place and cut out the fabric adding 2–3cm (¾–1¼in) extra round the edges for the seam allowance – enough for a double fold hem.

Sew the side edges

Fold over the edges 1cm (⅜in) and fold again. Pin in place and sew. Use a straight stitch in matching thread or, to make a feature of the edging, sew in a contrasting colour in zigzag or herringbone stitch.

Sew all around the edge of the apron, turning the corners in neatly. Finish off the end of the seams using the reverse motion on your machine.

Make a kangaroo pocket

Decide how big a pocket you want on the front of your apron (you don't have to have one at all for a really simple design). Cut out an oblong shape, slightly narrower than the width of the apron and to the depth you want for your pocket.

Fold over and sew a double hem on the top edge. Lay the pocket right side up on top of the apron, positioning it centrally and at a comfortable point for access with your hands.

Fold in a seam allowance on the three closed sides and pin in place.

Sew around (leaving the top open obviously!). To prevent the pocket sagging and to create two smaller pockets, sew a double row of stitches up the middle of the pouch.

Attach the ties

Hold the apron up to yourself to see how much ribbon you need round your neck. Cut the ribbon to the required length and turn under a narrow fold at each end. Stitch securely to either side of the top of your apron at the corners.

Cut two matching ties for the waist and sew these to the sides, again with a small hem, just below where the apron narrows into the bib. Pink the open ends of each tie to stop fraying.

Iron the apron and you're done!

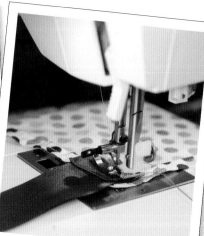

Sloe gin

There is nothing like the excitement of scrabbling about in hedgerows and screaming 'stop the car!' during the sloe season. These fruits look a bit like blueberries but actually are quite hard, have stones and are in the plum family. They ripen in late autumn. They are not for eating, but who cares when you can make the wonderful liqueur, sloe gin?

Picking sloes

Experts advise picking sloes after the first frost, but you risk there being none left if you wait too long. Frost helps soften the fruit and split it, avoiding the need to prick the sloes before starting the gin. You can put them in a freezer bag in the freezer for a few days, but the pricking process is all part of the fun.

Sloes are ripe when they are a deep blueberry colour and have a frosty opacity. When you squeeze them they should be a bit soft – you don't want bullets.

Making the sloe gin

If the frost hasn't done it for you, prick each sloe twice with a darning needle, then put them into a clean wine bottle. When it is half full, add 75–115g (2¾–4oz) of sugar depending how sweet you like it.

Fill up the bottle with gin. Any old gin will do – a supermarket own label 37.5 per cent proof gin will do just fine. Make sure the screw-cap or cork is pushed in securely and give it a good shake to disperse the sugar. Shake the bottle several times over the next week, as the sugar sinks to the bottom.

When the sugar is finally dissolved, stick the gin away in a dark cupboard and leave it alone.

When will it be ready?

Give it a year – or at least six months. It tastes even better after a year or more. Have a sip after several months to check the sweetness and if it is too sharp add some more sugar and keep shaking for a few days, then stick it back in the cupboard.

When it tastes about right, strain it through a bit of muslin (cheesecloth) and dispose of the sloes. They will have imparted the beautiful rose pink colour that characterizes this delicious drink.

Label each bottle with the date and where you found the sloes.

Sloe gin is delicious, if lethal. Your head might not thank you the next day, but you will surely get hooked on the ritual.

Mend It! Around the house

Fitting a new oven seal

A simple but essential task to keep your oven operating properly.

Find the right part

Check you can get the correct spare for your oven. Use your manufacturers' website, plus there are many spares suppliers online.

To fit, simply unhook the existing seal from each corner and discard. Clean around the area to remove any trapped grease. Hook the new seal in its place.

You can also use a universal oven door seal kit. This is a seal you cut to size. This option is usually only possible where there is a single hook hole in each corner. Many ovens have double hook holes at each corner and only work with the manufacturer's part.

Unblocking a sink

Simple tips for unblocking drains without using damaging chemicals, or paying a plumber.

Boiling water may do the trick

But you need to do some pre-prep if the sink is already full of cold, greasy water.

Bale out the sink then soak up as much accessible water as possible from the plughole with a large sponge. You can also pour a little washing-up liquid down the plughole and let it penetrate for 15 minutes before adding the boiling water.

Try a plunger

You don't have to drain the sink to use a plunger, but it is a good idea to block the overflow. Hold a wet cloth over the overflow with one hand while plunging with the other. Alternatively, dry the overflow area and seal with duct tape.

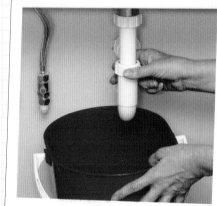
Remove the trap under the sink

Last resorts

If things are really bad you will need a drain auger, sometimes called a plumber's snake. This snakes down the pipe and clears the blockage. If you don't want to buy one you can often find them in tool hire shops.

Depending on where the blockage is you may need to remove the trap, the section of pipe under the sink, which unscrews at both ends to give you access.

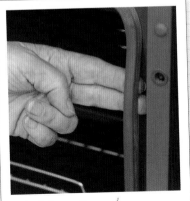
Unhook the existing seal

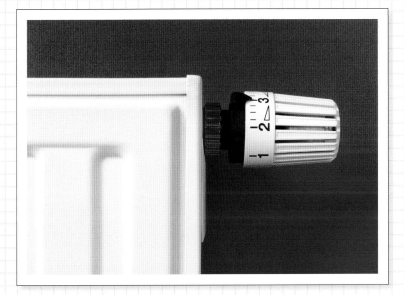

Tip

Shut curtains in the evenings. Consider fitting inter-linings to curtains. These are thicker linings of blanket-type material that are more effective at keeping out the cold.

Get heat where you need it

One of the easiest DIY jobs is to fit foil behind radiators, with the dull surface against the wall. This reflects the heat back into the room and makes radiators more efficient. You can use cooking foil but this is fragile and easily tears when fitting. Much better to invest in radiator foil, which is tougher and sometimes comes in a kit with the two-sided tape needed to fit it.

All you have to do is cut the foil to shape, put the tape on the top and bottom edges, feed it behind the radiator between the wall brackets and fix in place.

Cutting down on draughts

Fifteen per cent of home energy is lost to draughts. Door and window seal reduces or eliminates them...

It is sticky backed and comes in rolls, so all you have to do is position it. If you have old or loose windows (that rattle in their frames) choose insulation that looks like a letter P or even a B in profile. This is 'plumper' and, when fixed into the inner edge of the frame tends to stop rattling as well as keep out draughts.

The bottom of doors and letter boxes can be made draught resistant using a brush-type insulation that hangs over any gaps.

No sweat quilt

Children grow out of sweatshirts at a rate of knots, so what do you do with them once they are past their sell by date? You can always turn them into dusters and cleaning cloths, but how about reinventing them into a lovely, cosy quilt to keep you warm on a winter's evening?

YOU WILL NEED

- Old sweatshirts
- Ruler
- Scissors
- Needle and thread
- A large fleece or more old sweatshirts for the backing
- Quilting pins
- Old buttons, wool (yarn) and felt for decoration

Decide on your pattern

Before you start to work on your design, see what materials and colours you have to work with. Sort the sweatshirts into piles according to colour, texture or patterns. The biggest pile will become your main colour, the rest will be fitted into your design.

The best way to create a design is to use graph paper so you can scale it down and check you have enough of each colour. Build up your pattern from the centre out.

Alternatively, you can build your design as you go by simply creating 30cm (12in) squares that you can join together. This method will give a more random design, but allows you to work with smaller squares and build up your confidence.

Cutting out

Use a ruler to get your sizing right. The old saying 'measure twice, cut once' is important if you don't want to run out of fabric.

Sewing the quilt

You can sew the quilt together by hand or use a machine. On a machine you will need a large stitch and loose tension so the fabric doesn't pull. If you are hand sewing it is best to use a backstitch to make sure that the stitching is firm enough.

Embellishing

Once you have completed the front of the quilt you can embellish it any way you like. For this quilt we used bits of felt, wool (yarn) and old buttons to create different patterns and motifs.

Embellish the quilt with wool stitching

Create the backing

To back your quilt, either buy some fleecing fabric or sew together lots of pieces of old sweatshirt in large squares, or even use an old curtain.

Lay the backing right side down on the floor and place the top piece right side up on top of it. Make sure the pieces are flat and matched evenly.

Tack (baste) the cover to the backing with a large running stitch or use quilting pins. Work from the centre outwards, smoothing the fabric as you go and making sure both layers are flat.

Sew the two pieces together. Do this by starting from the middle and working outwards. You can sew around the inside or outside of your squares – or if you prefer, work a different pattern such as crossing diagonals across the quilt to create diamonds. It is important to do this to anchor the top to the bottom.

The nice thing about this quilt is that you don't need to buy any wadding (batting), as the sweatshirts are thick enough to do this job on their own.

Finishing off

When you have sewn the front and back you need to finish off the edges. For this quilt we made tassels out of old wool (yarn) and sewed the edges with blanket stitch for a chic, homespun look.

Make tassels out of old wool

Tips

- Why not make a memory quilt using the kids' old clothes?
- Make your quilt special by adding bits of old jewellery, buttons or beads.

WINTER

BANISH THOSE WINTER CHILLS BY KITTING A DRAUGHT
EXCLUDER – THEN STAY WARM IN BED WITH A HOT WATER
BOTTLE IN A COVER MADE FROM AN OLD SWEATER.
AND AS YOU DAYDREAM OF SUMMER HOLIDAYS, FOLLOW
OUR MONEY-SAVING IDEAS FOR USING UP LEFTOVERS IN
WINTER WARMING RECIPES.

Top tips for cooking with leftovers

We throw away tons of food waste every year. This is a hidden cost to the average family, not to mention the environmental impact. Stopping this waste would not only save the average family a significant amount of money each month, it would also be beneficial for the environment.

Here are our tips for you to do your bit to cut down food waste and help the environment and your pocket

1. Understand packaging sell by instructions

The most important usage direction on food packaging is the 'use by' date and food should not be eaten after this date. 'Best by' is nothing to do with safety, but is a measure of quality, so food is still safe after this date but may have lost some flavour and texture. The exception to this is eggs – see below. The third label you find on packs is 'Display until' – you can ignore this as it is for shop staff not consumers.

HOW TO CHECK FRESHNESS IN EGGS
- Fill a fairly deep bowl with water and gently lower the egg into the water.
- If it is very fresh it will sink to the bottom and lie flat. This is because the air sac in the egg is quite small.
- As the egg loses freshness more air enters it.
- If it stands upright, with the narrow end towards the bottom. It should be still OK to consume.
- If it floats fully in the water don't eat it, as it will most likely be bad.

2. Use up old raw vegetables in stews

Vegetables that no longer look lush and fresh can still be useful. (We are not talking about fossilized remains from the bottom of the chiller drawer – just veg that looks a bit sad and limp.) Chop them up and use them in soups and stocks or to bulk out a casserole.

If, like most of us, you always have more celery than you need, chop the rest and freeze it. Freezing makes it soggy – but that won't matter when you add it to soups and stews. The same applies to onions.

3. Tasty treats from leftover cooked vegetables

Leftover mashed potato should never be chucked, as you are missing out on a treat – potato cakes. All it takes is some flour, a bit of rolling and a quick bake in the oven and you can eat them hot with butter.

Another way to use up leftover mashed potato is to combine it with leftover cabbage or other vegetables to make 'Bubble and squeak'. Just mix it all up, season and fry in a pan until it bubbles and squeaks and gets brown underneath, then flip it over and brown the other side.

4. Use up fruit in cakes

Old bruised apples and pears that aren't attractive enough to eat raw can make a delicious moist cake. For a real feast, a boiled orange mixed with eggs, sugar, chocolate and flour is about the fastest thing in the world to make and turns out a genuinely gorgeous cake. Banana bread – a constant winner – is perfect for using up over-ripe bananas.

5. Make your own meat stock

Adding real, home-made stock makes a huge difference to your cooking.

You can make stock from leftover meat and poultry bones. Methods are slightly different for raw and cooked bones. A good cookbook will show you how.

6. Make and freeze breadcrumbs

When you get to the end of the loaf and it is getting a bit stale just pop in a food processor and make breadcrumbs. Put these in small bags and stick them in the freezer to use when you need them. They are great for a crusty topping, to mix with egg for a coating for fishcakes or meat cutlets, to thicken up soups and stews.

7. Leftover pasta

This is one of the most frequently thrown out foods. You can avoid waste by getting your portions right – allow 75–100g (2¾–3½oz) per person. If you do over-cater, toss it in some olive oil and put it in a plastic bag in the refrigerator, ready to make a delicious meal the next day. For a frittata just add beaten eggs and some garlic, fried onions or some leftover salami or sausage. Or if you have more time and ingredients, make a pasticcio (pasta bake). If you keep the pasta well oiled in a bag so it stays soft and doesn't stick together you can also use it cold in a salad.

8. Use the Internet

If you have a few odd ingredients and don't know what to do with them, try listing them in a search engine online and see what recipes come up. We have discovered some amazing ideas this way.

Knit a draught excluder

Keep the wind from getting under the door with this simple, but effective draught excluder. If you can do stocking (stockinette) stitch, know how to cast (bind) on and off and increase/decrease, you can make this.

YOU WILL NEED

- 150g (5oz) of chunky knit (bulky weight) yarn (we used Patons Shadow Tweed)
- Pair of 6mm (US size 10) knitting needles
- Needle and thread
- Polyester toy stuffing
- Some trimming or buttons to finish

Make the body

Cast (bind) on 40 stitches and knit in stocking (stockinette) stitch – knit one row, purl one row – to fit the required width of your door. This one was 75cm (29½in) long. Cast (bind) off.

Make the two end pieces

Cast (bind) on 4 stitches. Knit a row. Purl a row.
Knit 1. Increase 1 stitch. Knit to last 2 stitches. Increase 1. Knit 1.
Purl a row.
Repeat these last two rows until you have 14 stitches on your needle.
Knit a row. Purl a row.
Knit 1 stitch. Knit 2 together. Knit to last 3 stitches. Knit 2 together. Knit 1.
Purl a row.
Repeat last two rows until you have 4 stitches left. Cast (bind) off.

Making up

Fold the main piece in half lengthways, right sides together and sew along the long side to make an open-ended tube.

Take one of the end pieces and with the right side facing inwards, sew it carefully onto one end. Turn the tube right side out.

Fill the tube with polyester toy stuffing. Sew the second end piece on to close the open end, right side out.

Finishing touches

We knitted a strip in the same yarn in rib stitch – cast (bind) on 14 stitches, knit 2, purl 2 to end of row and repeat row as purl 2 knit 2 etc. Continue until the strip is long enough to go around the tube. Cast (bind) off. Sew this in place and add a decorative button or brooch in a contrasting colour.

Alternative

If you don't want to make the end pieces, you can make your tube 15cm (6in) longer and tie the first open end with ribbon like a Christmas cracker. Fill the tube with polyester toy stuffing and tie the other end to match.

Top tips for growing winter vegetables indoors

There is no need to give up on home grown additions to your food supply, even if it is snowing a blizzard outside, when you can create your own indoor vegetable garden.

1. Containers

Space can be an issue when 'gardening' indoors, so divide the vegetables up into small pots and tubs. Go for attractive containers (or decorate them) so your veg doesn't look out of place in the dining room or sitting room.

Container depth is more important than width (for retaining moisture and leaving room for roots). The air in your home will be relatively dry – particularly if the central heating is on – and veg won't do well in rooms that are too warm. Invest in moisture-retaining compost and don't over water, in case it leaks and stains floors.

Smaller containers will also be easier to manoeuvre and rotate so that your plants get a good share of the available daylight.

2. Light

Place your containers where they will get the most natural light possible. Conservatories are an obvious place, and you should get good results in loft conversions with large dormer or Velux windows. On warmer, sunnier days think about ventilation as well as light.

Even the most enthusiastic winter veg may need some artificial light. Take particular care if you plan to grow your veg from seedlings, as they can become rather long and weak if they are struggling to get enough light during the day, or the light source is narrow and high up. It is worth investing in proper grow bulbs that emit full spectrum light.

3. What to grow
Herbs and lettuces are obvious choices. But don't stop there. Try other leafy greens, (bell) peppers, chillies, beans, courgettes (zucchini) and garlic greens (you harvest the shoots rather than wait for the bulbs – they are great diced in soups and stews or added to mayonnaise).

Indoor varieties of radish grow really quickly, as do mini varieties of cucumbers and peas.

Cherry tomatoes look pretty, as well as working well on window sills. Full-size tomato plants need to be tethered to something fairly substantial to stop the pot falling over (and they will definitely need a grow bulb).

Protecting plants
Plastic cloche pots can also be used indoors to give your seedlings a boost and protect from draughts.

Hot water bottle cover

We all love curling up with a hot water bottle when it is cold. This one is made from an old sweatshirt that would otherwise have been thrown away.

YOU WILL NEED

- Hot water bottle
- Paper to make a pattern
- Old sweatshirt
- Scissors
- Dressmaking pins
- Black felt, wool (yarn) and ribbon to decorate
- Sewing machine and thread

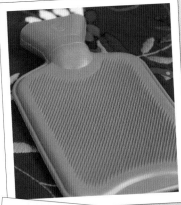

Create a template

For the front – lay your hot water bottle on a piece of paper and draw round it, allowing about 2.5cm (1in) all the way round. Cut out the shape. For the back – copy this shape two more times. With the first shape make a mark two thirds down from the top and cut along this line. Take the second shape and repeat as above, but this time making a mark two thirds up from the bottom and cut along the line. (The idea is to have an overlap between the two pieces of fabric.)

Pin on the templates

Cutting out

Cut the sweatshirt in half, removing the front from the back and lay it flat – right sides up. Pin on the templates, using the bottom welt of the sweatshirt for the flap at the back. Cut your shapes out.

Decorate the cover

Before sewing up the cover, why not add some decoration? For this cover, we cut black felt in the shape of a Scottie dog (see **Templates** section) and appliquéd it on with blanket stitch and added a small bow.

Tip

Use fabric glue or Bondaweb to stick the appliqué in place before stitching it.

Stitching up

Take the front and lay it down right side up. Take the two back pieces and lay them wrong side down on top of the front piece. Overlap the back pieces to create a flap.

Stitch all the way round the outer edge, allowing about 1.5cm (⅝in) for the seam allowance. Turn right side out.

To finish off, blanket stitch around the edge and you have a lovely little hot water bottle cover to add some glamour to those cold winter nights.

Alternative version from an old jumper

Using the same approach you can make this cover from an old knitted jumper or any oddments of fabricthat you already have, you can also make it from an old knitted jumper, as shown opposite.

You will need to make sure that the jumper doesn't fray or unravel in the making process. This is easily done by marking out the shape of your hot water bottle (plus a 1cm (⅜in) seam allowance) on the wrong side of the fabric with a marker and then stitching around this shape using the zigzag stitch on your sewing machine. This will hold the knitting stitches together while you make up the cover.

Once it is complete you can either bind the raw edges on the inside with seam binding or whiz around the edges with another round of zigzag stitch.

Use blanket stitch to edge the cover

Make a coffee table out of an old door

We love making things from unwanted leftovers. This coffee table was made by Hilary's son from stuff he found lying around in the garage and greenhouse.

'I'm delighted the making gene is still alive and kicking in my family and has been passed to my son. I was looking for a table for the summer house and he created this masterpiece with an old cupboard door and some storage boxes from the greenhouse.'
Hilary

YOU WILL NEED

- Old door
- 2–4 old wooden boxes
- Coarse-grade sandpaper
- Paintbrush
- Satin wood (eggshell) or emulsion (latex) paint
- Screwdriver and screws

Finding your wood

Don't spend a fortune buying wood, ask your friends and family or check out junk shops, skips, or reclamation yards. You'll find that hunting for a piece is half the fun!

Prepping and painting

Remove any sticking out nails from the door and boxes. You may want to leave any fittings as these can add character – but remember to cover them with masking tape when you paint the door.

Wash down the wood and then give it a quick rub over with an electric sander or sandpaper, so you have a smooth surface to work with.

Apply a coat of paint to the door and boxes. For a distressed finish, use satinwood or emulsion. Leave to dry thoroughly.

Distressing the wood

Once the paint has dried, distress the wood by using sandpaper to rub it down. Don't be too thorough or you will end up with bare wood again. You want a distressed, whitewashed (limed) effect.

Assembling the table

Put the boxes in position and lay the door on top. Screw the door to the boxes. You may need another person to help you keep the pieces in place while you drill. You could just nail the pieces together, but screws will hold better.

CHRISTMAS

THERE'S NOTHING BETTER THAN A HOUSE DECORATED WITH HOME-MADE CHRISTMAS CRAFTS. MAKING CARDS, BISCUITS AND TREE DECORATIONS ARE A GREAT WAY TO KEEP THE KIDS BUSY, TOO!

Christmas cards

The secret to handmade Christmas cards is to come up with designs you can 'mass produce'. Card blanks with matching envelopes are widely available and the following ideas use materials and tools that you may already have or are easy to get.

Collage cards

This idea uses scrap paper and fabric to get the handmade look on a 'production line'.

YOU WILL NEED

- Scissors
- Remnant fabric (such as gold or silver brocade)
- Metallic tissue paper (such as saved Christmas wrapping)
- Spray adhesive glue

Cut out star shapes from the fabric brocade. These can be uneven – perfection is not the goal.

Cut or tear blocks of the metallic tissue paper.

In a protected space (use an old cereal packet to create a shelter for spraying the glue) briefly spray the underside of the fabric and tissue paper with the adhesive glue.

Position the shapes where you like on the card to produce your own impression of a starry night.

Glitter and glue collage

Always use fine glitters and solvent-based or hobby glue. These glues don't buckle the cards and the fine glitters stick better and produce the most intense effects. Here is one of our ideas – but let your own imagination take over.

YOU WILL NEED

- Scissors
- Scrap paper
- Spray adhesive glue
- Glue (such as hobby glue)
- Fine glitter

Tear or cut your paper. But you can use old wrapping paper or images from magazines and newspapers.

Briefly spray the paper pieces with adhesive glue in a shelter. Stick them into position on your card – and think about using the back as well.

Apply some hobby glue in any pattern wherever you like on your card. Shake on the fine glitter as abundantly as you can to give a really rich feel. Shake off the excess and replace in the glitter container.

Leave to dry completely – this may take overnight.

Tip

Use a solvent-based glitter glue made with fine glitter. Children's glitter glue is water-based and will buckle the card if used.

Make your own mincemeat

Home-made mincemeat tastes much better than manufactured versions. It is incredibly easy and makes a lovely Christmas gift. This recipe uses no horrid candied peel, the apples are Cox's as they are more fragrant than sour Bramleys, and orange zest plays a starring role.

Like many Christmas specialities, you can make it months ahead – but also on the day you need to use it.

YOU WILL NEED

- 300g (10½oz) Cox's apples (peeled, cored and chopped weight)
- 150g (5oz) shredded vegetable suet
- 225g (8oz) raisins
- 150g (5oz) sultanas
- 150g (5oz) currants
- 150g (5oz) other dried mixed fruit – include soft-dried apricots chopped small, blueberries, for colour throw in a few cranberries
- 225g (8oz) soft brown sugar
- Grated zest of 2 oranges
- Grated zest and juice of 1 lemon
- 50g (2oz) whole almonds, chopped
- 3 teaspoons mixed ground spice
- ½ teaspoon cinnamon
- A very good grating of nutmeg
- 75ml (5 tablespoons) brandy

Makes 4 x 450g (1lb) jars

Set the oven to its lowest temperature – around 50°C/120°F.

In a large heatproof bowl mix together all the ingredients (except the brandy) and leave them to stand for a while to get used to each other.

Place the bowl into the warm oven for about 3 hours. Stir it a couple of times. The suet will melt throughout the ingredients.

Bring the mixture out of the oven to cool. When it is back to room temperature, stir in the brandy.

Pack in jars that have been sterilized. When filled, cover with waxed discs and seal.

Lovely to use immediately for pies, tarts and turnovers. Unopened you can store the mincemeat for a year. Once open, use within a month.

Tip
Make mince pies with all butter shortcrust pastry with added fresh orange zest – delicious!

Salt dough decorations

For cheap Christmas decorations, or a more creative way to decorate your tree, then look no further than this great basic salt dough recipe.

YOU WILL NEED

- 250g (9oz) plain flour
- 275g (10oz) table salt
- 250ml (9fl oz) water
- Cookie cutters
- Decorations – glass gems or mirror pieces
- Paint (acrylic paints work well)
- Glue
- Glitter
- Ribbon

Make the dough

Put all the dry ingredients into a mixing bowl. Gradually add the water, mixing to a soft dough and knead for 10 minutes.

Leave the dough to stand for about 20 minutes before working with it.

While the dough rests, cover two large baking trays with greaseproof (wax) paper.

Cut out your shapes

Place the dough on a floured work surface and roll out to a thickness of 5mm–1cm (³⁄₁₆–⅛in) thick. Use cookie cutters to cut out shapes.

While the dough is still pliable, make a hole in each shape to allow for a ribbon for hanging. Don't make the hole too small or you won't be able to get the ribbon through. You can also create a relief effect at this stage by using a chopstick to make indentations, or for extra sparkle press glass gems or even some mirror pieces into the dough.

Dry your decorations

Transfer the shapes to the baking trays and dry in a very cool oven (110°C/225°F/Gas Mark ¼) for 2–3 hours until they they are completely dried out.

You can save on energy by leaving the dough to dry naturally, but it can take 48 hours for the decorations to dry. If you are in a real rush pop them in a microwave for 2–3 minutes.

Decorate the shapes

Once your shapes are completely cool you can use any paint or glitter and glue to make them look pretty. Acrylic paints work well as they give a nice smooth finish.

Once the decorations are dry, thread through the ribbon and hang on the Christmas tree or around the house for a wonderfully festive feel.

Tips

- Avoid the temptation to turn up the oven heat to save time... it won't. All it will do is cause the dough to bubble and crack!
- Unused dough can be stored in the refrigerator, in an airtight container or clingfilm (plastic wrap), for up to a week.

Festive foliage wreath

Seasonal wreathes are very expensive – so why not make your own? A tramp round the garden or the countryside and a rummage in the Christmas decorations box can probably yield most of what you need.

YOU WILL NEED

- Wire coat hanger
- Large bag of ivy
- Large bag of holly with berries
- Decorations – baubles, bells, pine cones, bunches of cinnamon sticks – or whatever you can find around the house
- Kitchen scissors and/or secateurs

Make the frame

Untwist the coat hanger and bend it into a circular shape. Remember once the foliage is wrapped around, it will be a bit bigger.

Add the foliage

Twist the ivy around the wire frame, going under and over, covering the wire to make the foundation for your wreath. When you are happy that it is bulky enough, add the holly, slotting the stems around the wreath.

Add decorations

Add any embellishments such as ribbons and baubles. We kept this one simple. Here are some suggestions:
- Tie baubles or bells in groups of three and secure with a little ribbon or wire.
- Add little bunches of cinnamon sticks for a lovely scent.
- Tie ribbons in knots or bows for a shabby chic effect.
- Twirl a long piece of wired ribbon around the whole wreath.

Tip

Wear a pair of gardening gloves as some foliage may irritate your hands.

Bend the coat hanger into a circular shape

Stained glass biscuits

These delicious biscuits are a great money saving way to decorate your Christmas tree.
They taste delicious, look fabulous and the kids will love making them.

YOU WILL NEED

- 175g (6oz) plain flour
- 100g (3½oz) butter, diced
- 1 teaspoon ground ginger
- Grated zest of 1 orange
- ½ teaspoon salt
- 50g (2oz) caster sugar
- 15ml (1 tablespoon) milk
- Cookie cutters
- 12 fruit-flavoured boiled sweets
- Icing (confectioner's) sugar to dust
  and decorate
- Sugar balls and ready-made icing
  to decorate
- Length of thin ribbon

Make the dough

Preheat your oven to 180°C/350°F/
Gas Mark 4.

Line two non-stick baking sheets
with baking parchment paper.

In a food processor, whiz together
the flour, butter, ginger, orange zest
and salt to create fine crumbs.
Pulse in the sugar and milk, then
turn out onto a floured surface
and knead briefly until smooth.
Wrap the dough in clingfilm
(plastic wrap) and chill in the
refrigerator for 30 minutes.

Flour the work surface and roll
out the dough to a thickness of
about 5mm (³⁄₁₆in).

Cut out your shapes

Use cookie cutters to stamp out
shapes and smaller cutters to cut
out the middles of each shape.

Re-roll the leftover dough and
repeat the cutting process.

Make a small hole in the top of
each biscuit to allow for ribbon to
hang it on the tree.

Carefully lift the shapes onto the
baking sheets.

Creating the stained glass

Roughly crush the coloured sweets
in their wrappers with a rolling pin
and put the pieces into the middles
of the biscuits.

Bake the biscuits

Bake for 15–20 minutes or until the
biscuits are golden brown and the
middles have melted.

Remove from the oven and leave to
cool on a wire rack.

Decorate the biscuits

When the biscuits are cool, you
can decorate them by sprinkling
with icing sugar and threading with
ribbon. Or, buy tubes of ready-made
icing and some edible sugar balls and
let your creativity flow.

Let the biscuits cool before decorating

VALENTINE'S DAY

THERE IS NO BETTER WAY TO SAY
'I LOVE YOU' THAN TO MAKE YOUR
BELOVED SOMETHING SPECIAL – EVEN IF IT
IS ONLY A CARD OR A COCKTAIL.

Handmade with love

On Valentine's day you want your card to your significant other to be unique, special... handmade with love. Here is a simple idea to inspire your own creation.

YOU WILL NEED

- Tissue paper – pink, red or a mix. Use saved tissue from presents and iron to reuse.
- Heart template (see **Templates** section)
- Spray adhesive glue
- Good quality card blank and envelope
- Tacky or paper glue
- Glitter, sequins or any other bits of sparkle

Make the heart

Cut ten 7.5cm (3in) squares of tissue paper. Layer them, fold them in half and trace the heart template onto them. Cut out and make sure the fold is kept creased.

Fix the heart to the card

Take one of the 10 hearts, spray one side with spray mount and position it flat on your card. Carefully dab a tiny line of tacky glue down the centre of the stuck heart and position the next tissue heart along the fold line. You are only gluing along the fold lines from now on.

Repeat until you have used all your layers. Let the glue dry then fan out the tissue layers for a beautiful 3-D heart effect.

Finishing touches

You can add tiny bits of glitter and/or sequins for added effect – but remember, less is more.

Add a great big X in glue on the card and sprinkle with red, fine glitter for a luscious kiss effect. Looks great beside a bottle of champagne!

Tip

Use the same concept to create a single rose... even a big bouquet!

Valentine's spritzer

Valentine's day is all about romance and romance is all about presentation. For that special evening you need something that looks, as well as tastes, romantic.

Champagne is the lovers' drink of choice, but it is pricey. A good sparkling wine is also expensive. And cheap fizzy wine taste like... cheap fizzy wine. So here are two alternatives that look and taste delicious.

Anne's Valentine spritzer

YOU WILL NEED

- 5–6 ice cubes
- 60ml (4 tablespoons) soda water, chilled
- 60ml (4 tablespoons) dry white wine, chilled
- 2 dashes Angostura bitters
- 1 dash Crème de Cassis (blackcurrant) or Crème de Fraise (strawberry)

Serves 1

Put the ice cubes in a tall glass and pour the soda water and dry white wine over them.

Add the bitters, and Crème de Cassis or Crème de Fraise. How much you add depends on how sweet you like things. Stir well and serve.

Venetian spritz

YOU WILL NEED

- 15ml (1 tablespoon) Campari
- 90ml (6 tablespoons) Prosecco
- 2 ice cubes

Serves 1

Mix the Campari and Prosecco straight into a chilled champagne flute. Garnish with ice or frozen fruit.

If you are looking for a cheaper alternative to Prosecco, the white wine and soda water mix from the spritzer recipe makes a good alternative.

PRESENTATION, PRESENTATION, PRESENTATION!

If you don't have champagne flutes or nice goblets, look out for them in junk shops. Wash and polish them until they gleam. You could also thread a few beads onto gold wire and wrap this around the stem of each glass.

And completely chill the glasses in the freezer before using. That is a nice touch.

Tip
Instead of ice you can use frozen strawberries, raspberries or cherries.

Melt your heart cake pops

Cake pops are a fun way to use up leftover cake. They are just cake crumbs bound together with buttercream frosting formed into a shape (mostly balls but in this case hearts), then coated with chocolate or candy coatings and decorated into pretty much anything you like.

YOU WILL NEED

- 250g (9oz) cake sponge – chocolate or vanilla
- 125g (4½oz) buttercream (2 parts icing (confectioner's) sugar to 1 part softened butter) flavoured to taste
- 450g (1lb) dark chocolate
- 425g (15oz) pink and/or red candy melts
- Small heart-shaped mould
- Lolly or pop sticks
- Cake decorations – sprinkles, edible glitter
- A block of polystyrene to hold the drying and finished cake pops
- Cellophane, foils and ribbons for final presentation

Makes 12

Make the basic cake pop base

Crumble the cake into a fine crumb. Mix in the buttercream until it is evenly distributed through the mix. It should still be crumbly.

Form the cake pops

Use a heart mould to shape your cake pops. Each heart should use about 30g (1oz) of mixture. Make sure the mixture is tightly packed.

Using one of your pop sticks, carefully make an indent into each heart at the pointy end to create a hole for the stick – about half the depth of the heart. Put onto a parchment-lined tray and refrigerate for up to 1 hour or freeze for 15 minutes.

Inserting the sticks

Melt the coatings – dark chocolate and pink or red candy melts.

Keeping your cake pop bases cold, pipe a little of the chocolate or candy melts into the indentation in the base and insert the stick. The cold of the cake will quickly set the stick into place, securing it well.

Coating the cake pops

Carefully dip the cake pop by its stick into the chocolate or candy coating. Be sure to cover right to the top of the stick to secure the pop in place. Gently tap the cake pop over the bowl to remove any excess coating. Aim for six in plain chocolate, six in pink or red.

Decorating

This is where you let your imagination rip. Add sprinkles while the coating is still wet. It will harden quickly as the pop is still frozen.

Let the coating harden and then use edible gold and silver icing or glitter to make your own design or spell out a special message.

Place upright in the polystyrene block to set completely.

Packaging

Make them look beautiful. Use cellophane, foil and ribbon to individually wrap your pops. Leave some unwrapped. You choose.

They can be presented as a bunch, in a champagne glass, stuck into romantically-wrapped polystyrene. Whatever looks good.

Use a heart mould to shape the pop

Recycled card gift boxes

These little boxes are a delight. They are really easy to make and don't even need any sticking or taping. Even better, they are kind to your purse as you make them from old greetings cards. You can make them as big or as small as you like and they make any gift look fabulous.

YOU WILL NEED

- Box template (see **Templates** section)
- Tracing paper for the template
- Scissors or craft knife
- Used greetings card or plain card
- Pencil
- Cutting board
- Ribbon and glitter to decorate

Trace the template

Trace around the template and cut out. With the card face up, place the template on top and draw around the shape with a pencil.

Cut out using scissors or a craft knife. (If you want to make the box bigger or smaller just scale up from this basic template.)

Score the folds

Place the card picture side up on the cutting board. Score along the fold lines – this will give you a nice neat/ sharp line when you come to fold the box into shape. Be very careful when you are scoring – don't press too hard, as you are only intending to give a slight indented line and not a complete cut through the card.

Make up the box

Using the scored lines as a guide, gently fold the card into a box shape. Fold each corner underneath the adjacent corner.

You can add some more decoration, such as glitter or bows, if you wish.

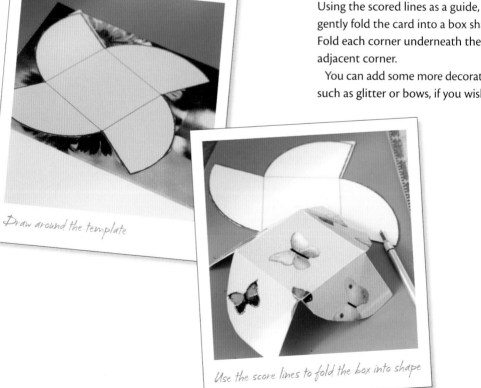

Draw around the template

Use the score lines to fold the box into shape

MOTHER'S DAY

SHOWING YOUR MUM HOW MUCH YOU CARE
WITH INEXPENSIVE TREATS AND THOUGHTFUL
GESTURES WILL MEAN MORE TO HER, AND
MAKE FOR A REALLY SPECIAL DAY.

Top tips for 5 things mums *don't* need for Mother's day

We have had our share of Mother's day gifts and the best ones didn't need a credit card. They include a bit of folded card with 'I love mum' scrawled inside, with the final 'm' in the word mum squished into place.

We've had artwork made of macaroni and lovingly, if erratically, plaited friendship bracelets strung with '18ct' plastic beads. Gifts like these are more precious than rubies.

So, if you want your mum's eyes to shine like diamonds on Mother's day, here is our Top 5 of what NOT to get her…

1. No store-bought cards
The greetings card industry spends a lot of money convincing us that only something fancy, and possibly with a microchip in it, will do. Don't believe them. The best cards are handmade.

2. Don't buy flowers

OK, they are a great fall back, but how about planting some seeds? Put them in a terracotta pot jazzed up with poster paint.

3. Don't buy jewellery

Any mum worth her salt will wear home-made jewellery with pride. Speaking of salt, our **Salt Dough Decorations** recipe can be repurposed for bangles, brooches, necklaces and earrings.

4. No meals out

Make mum dinner instead or if that is too ambitious serve her breakfast in bed. Try eggy toast (French toast). Mix an egg, a little milk, salt and pepper in a shallow bowl. Soak a slice of bread in the mixture and lightly fry both sides until golden brown. Delicious!

5. No store-bought perfume

Older children can try their hand at making perfume – try a simple solid perfume by combining melted beeswax with almond oil and an essential oil, such as rose. Or just run mum a nice bath and let her soak in peace.

And finally, give mum the thing money can't buy...

Spend a little time with her. Even if that means being dragged round a garden centre or watching a weepy movie. A chat over breakfast and a hug after tea mean more than anything that comes with a big bow and shiny wrapping paper.

Home-made perfume

Mixing your own perfume sounds exotic but it is also very easy, highly personal, satisfying and, even with pure essential oils, only costs half what you would spend on a commercial perfume.

YOU WILL NEED

- 4–6 different essential oils
- Cotton swabs/buds
- Glass jar
- Notepad and pen
- Glass dropper
- Glass bottle to experiment with your perfume notes
- 75ml (5 tablespoons) alcohol (pure vodka is best, or use brandy)
- 30ml (2 tablespoons) distilled or spring water
- Coffee filter
- Glass bottle for your perfume (a dark colour protects the scent)

DECIDE ON YOUR NOTES

Base notes stay on your skin the longest and become stronger as the others fade. Try cinnamon, patchouli or vanilla.

Middle notes become evident after the top note has faded: usually 30 minutes or so after applying the perfume. Some good middle notes are nutmeg, geranium and ylang-ylang.

A top note is most evident when you first apply the perfume. Citrus and floral scents make good top notes.

A bridge note ties the others together. Vanilla and lavender are good examples.

Creating your scent

Choose oils to blend from base, middle, top and bridging notes.

Dip a clean cotton bud into the first essential oil. Squeeze any excess oil from the swab on the lip of the oil bottle. Put the cotton bud in the glass jar.

Repeat for each oil you want to blend – ending up with as many as six individually scented cotton buds in the jar. Write down each oil you use. Leave for about 5 minutes.

Sniff the air above the jar. This will be the scent blend in its early stage of development. Take notes on your thoughts about it. Is one oil overpowering the others? Do two of them seem too similar to tell apart? Make any corrections.

Bottling the scent

Once you are happy with the blend, put several drops of the base note into a glass bottle. Add the other notes a few drops at a time, sniffing after each addition until you reach a balance you like. Use at least 25 drops in total.

Add the alcohol and water. Shake vigorously for several minutes to mix the ingredients.

Seal and leave in a cool, dark place. After a few hours, open and smell the blend again.

Adjust the blend if you like, then seal the bottle and leave in a cool, dark place for 48 hours. Open and smell again. You can keep adjusting the blend, leaving the bottle each time to mature.

Pour the mixture through a coffee filter into a perfume bottle.

Make your own hand cream

Hand cream is very simple and quick to make – and good for your skin. There are no preservatives, so make it in small batches and if you are giving it as a gift, write a use-by date on the label. This version lasts 3–4 weeks at room temperature. There are many suppliers of specialist ingredients online.

YOU WILL NEED

- 60ml (4 tablespoons) emulsifying wax or beeswax
- 6.5ml (¼ teaspoon) almond oil
- 300ml (10fl oz) hot water – about 60°C/140°F
- 24–36 drops essential oil
- 500ml (18fl oz) capacity glass jar
- Adhesive labels

Heat the wax

Combine the emulsifying wax and almond oil and heat to about 70°C/158°F. A microwave oven is useful for this.

Heat the water

Gently heat the water, which can also be done in a microwave oven to about 60°C/140°F.

Choose your scent

While the water is heating, add essential oil drops to the blended oil and emulsifying wax. Use a single oil such as rose or lavender, or try your own personal blend.

Add the heated water (the mix will turn milky white) and stir well. You now have an emulsion (that is what the emulsifying wax does).

Jar and label the hand cream

Pour it into a clean glass jar and let it cool and set completely.

Make one large jar, or divide into smaller jars for gifts. Add a special message on a label if you wish, and don't forget the use-by date!

Try your own blend of essential oils

Tip

Try making your own labels using your printer for a handmade touch.

Handmade truffles

Truffles are a special treat and there is no better excuse to make and give them than on Mother's day. This is a basic recipe with three coatings, but by adding or changing a few ingredients, you could make your mum an impressive selection.

YOU WILL NEED

- 200g (7oz) dark chocolate (70 per cent cocoa solids)
- 200ml (7fl oz) double cream
- 40g (1½oz) unsalted butter
- 15–30ml (1–2 tablespoons) brandy or Grand Marnier (optional)

Makes 20 truffles

For the coatings

Use all or any of these:
- Cocoa powder
- Toasted and finely chopped almonds
- Grated milk chocolate

Presentation

- Confectionery cases (optional)
- Something lovely to pack them in – box, tin, ceramic or glass container – or a cellophane bag tied with a colourful bow

Make the truffle mixture

Melt the chocolate over a *baine marie* or double boiler.

Put the cream and butter in a pan and heat gently – be careful not to boil the mixture.

Cool both, then quickly combine them. Keep beating until the mix is glossy. Beat in your alcohol, if using.

Leave the mixture to set in the refrigerator for up to 4 hours.

Make the balls

Take the mixture out of the refrigerator and leave for 5 minutes. Line a large baking tray with greaseproof paper.

To shape the truffles, take a good teaspoonful of the mix and roll it into an even ball. Place the ball onto the tray. Repeat until you have used all the mix. This is quite messy, so do all your truffles before starting to coat them.

Roll the truffles in their coatings

For the coatings

If you are using grated milk chocolate, grate and leave in the refrigerator for 15 minutes to chill. Prepare your almonds and sieve your cocoa powder on separate plates.

Working quickly, roll your truffles in their coatings and put them into small confectionary cases or pack however you like into your gift container. These will keep for a couple of weeks in a refrigerator and for a few months in a freezer.

Give, eat and make again!

Personalize a potted plant

A well placed plant pot can make a garden or a room look a million dollars – but they only need to cost a few pennies. With a little creative know-how you can create your own cheerful pots that will make your mum smile.

YOU WILL NEED
- Old terracotta plant pot
- PVA glue
- Paintbrush
- Polyurethane varnish
- Old book paper, sheet music or images (or specialist découpage paper)

Prepare the pot
Take an old terracotta plant pot and clean it thoroughly to remove any excess dirt or grease. Allow to dry.

Apply the decoration
Paint a thin coat of watered down PVA glue over the pot to prime it. Take your chosen paper and tear it into small squares.

Using PVA glue, stick the paper pieces to the pot. Keep attaching them and overlapping them until you get the result you want. Allow to dry thoroughly.

Apply a thin coat of polyurethane varnish to seal the surface and keep it nice and waterproof.

Finishing touches
Plant the pot with a bulb or some seeds, or fill it with mum's favourite chocolates.

Decorate with sheet music from a favourite song

Tip
These pots also make great desk tidies for pencils or paintbrushes.

EASTER

CELEBRATED WITH CHICKENS, EGGS, SPRING FLOWERS, RABBITS AND CHOCOLATE – THESE EASTER PROJECTS ARE FUN FOR THE WHOLE FAMILY TO ENJOY.

Top tips for planning an egg hunt

Children love Easter egg hunts and there are lots of different ways to do them, depending on your budget and the time and energy you have.

1. The demolition derby approach

If you have a big garden, or just a few children, and don't mind them creating havoc, buy some small chocolate eggs, hide them round the garden and get the kids to find them.

If you don't want your flower beds destroyed, mark out some 'No go' areas. Or, minimize the destruction by hiding the eggs in safe places or organizing the hunt in a local park.

If there is a big age gap between the children, give the little ones a head start or the older ones will grab the lot!

All you need are the eggs, fine weather and some baskets, egg boxes or small bags for each child to collect their eggs.

2. The egg-head's version

This involves the children using their brains. The disadvantage is you have to use *your* brain too – to dream up the clues to where the eggs are hidden.

If you are feeling creative you can make rhyming clues or picture clues. The first clue is handed to everyone. When they solve it and get to the right place they will find the second clue that leads to the third and so on.

Children are pretty good at cracking the clues and if they are slightly cryptic they will try different ideas out, rather than all racing along together and dive-bombing the clue location.

Use something to hold the clues, such as empty matchboxes or upturned eggcups. This stops them blowing away and makes it more obvious when a child finds them.

3. Treasure island hunt

If your mapping skills are up to it and you have the patience, turn the hunt area into a treasure island and draw a map with all the egg locations on it. This will test the children's map-reading skills. And they can dress up as pirates.

4. Lazy version

If you don't have time or inclination for clue-writing and planning, you can always hitch your wagon to an organized hunt, or team up with other parents to share the load.

5. Make it special

After the hunt, have an Easter bunny picnic. If it is too cold to do it outdoors, put a cloth on the kitchen floor and give everyone cushions to sit on. Serve Easter themed cupcakes, egg soldiers and mini chocolate bunnies.

Gift boxes for spring chickens

These little boxes are easy to make and versatile to use. Filled with sweeties or mini chocolate eggs they make great gifts or party favours for the kids at Easter, or they can be personalized as gifts on the dining table for a festive meal.

YOU WILL NEED

- Box template (see **Templates** section)
- Tracing paper for the template
- Scissors or craft knife
- Used birthday card or plain card
- Ruler
- Pencil
- Cutting board
- Glue
- Ribbon and glitter to decorate

Trace the template

Trace around the template and cut out. With the card face up, place the template on top and draw around the shape with a pencil. Cut out your shape using scissors or a craft knife.

Score the folds

Place the card picture side up on the cutting board. Score the fold lines – this will give you a nice neat/sharp line when you come to fold the box into shape.

Be very careful when you are scoring – don't press too hard as you are only intending to give a slight indented line and not completely cut through the card.

Make up the box

Using the scored lines as a guide, gently fold the box into shape. Glue the tab marked **A** to the edges marked **B** and leave to dry.
You can leave it plain or add ribbons, glitter and sparkles.

Draw around the template

Use scored lines to fold the box into shape

Elegant egg candles

These little candles are perfect for Easter. You can make them in different colours and even use up the ends of old candles. They are really easy to do and make great table decorations.

YOU WILL NEED

- Large brown eggs or duck eggs
- Egg topper
- Soap
- Acrylic paint
- Wicks dipped in wax
- Toothpicks or lolly sticks
- A block of white beeswax (or bits of old candles to melt down)
- Double boiler, to melt the wax

Clean the eggshells

Remove the top from the raw eggs with an egg topper. Empty the contents into a bowl – omelettes tonight? Wash the eggshells in soapy water and let them dry completely. *Note: Be sure to wash your hands thoroughly whenever handling raw eggs.*

Prepare and paint the shells

Using your fingers, gently break the edges of the eggshells to make them shallower and create a jagged look. (The eggshell will blacken if it curves over the top of a lit wick.) Paint the **inside** of each shell with acrylic paint – you can paint them all the same colour or do each shell in a different hue if you like.

Add the wicks

Tie each wick to a toothpick or lolly stick and suspend it across the top of the eggshell.

Melt the wax

Place the wax in the smaller inner pan of the double boiler and let it melt over a medium heat. Stir occasionally with an old wooden spoon. Don't leave it unattended as it is flammable.

Add the wax

Carefully pour the melted wax into the eggshells, almost to the top. The wax when it dries will appear to take on the colour of the painted insides.

Let the wax cool for several hours. Trim the wicks 6mm (¼in) above the surface.

Tip

If you haven't got a double boiler, use an old high-sided pan placed inside a larger pan. An old milk pan works well as it has a lip for pouring.

Hop-along bunny tablecloth

We all have those moments when the red wine gets spilt or the tomato ketchup is dribbled across the tablecloth. These sorts of stains usually spell the end of the tablecloth, but with a little creativity and some well placed appliqué, tablecloths can be given a second lease of life.

YOU WILL NEED

- Old tablecloth
- Rabbit templates (see **Templates** section)
- Old shirts
- Pencil
- Scissors
- Needle and thread
- Iron-on adhesive, such as Bondaweb
- Iron and ironing board
- Embroidery silk and old buttons for decoration

Sort out your fabric

Make sure all the fabric you are going to use is washed and ironed.

Create a template

You can use the templates provided at the back of this book or create your own Easter design if you wish. Lay the templates onto the shirt fabric and draw around them. Cut out with scissors. Continue until you have all the pieces for your design.

Lay the pieces out on the tablecloth, making sure you cover up any stains or tears.

Attach the fabric pieces

Before you start sewing, 'glue' your fabric templates to the tablecloth with a paper based, double-sided iron-on adhesive such as Bondaweb.

Lay the adhesive sheet out and draw around the original fabric shapes. Following the instructions, attach the adhesive to the template.

Trim around the shape to make sure the pieces match and remove the paper backing. This will leave a sticky side that can be laid face down on the cloth in the chosen position. Iron the fabric shape into place.

Repeat this until all the fabric pieces are positioned and fixed to the tablecloth.

Secure the appliqué shapes

Either hand sew around the shapes with a needle and embroidery cotton, or use a machine embroidery stitch to go neatly around the edges.

Make sure each piece is edged thoroughly so it won't fray.

Finishing off

Once all the applique shapes are secured in place you can decorate them with buttons or embroider extra detail. We used pink embroidery silk for our rabbits' eyes and noses and old shirt buttons as tails, and to create the ground.

Easter baking – hot cross buns

There is something special about making your own hot cross buns and filling the house with the smell of spice, citrus and warm yeasty baking. Instead of mixed peel this recipe includes fresh orange zest.

YOU WILL NEED

For the buns
- 450g (1lb) strong white bread flour
- 1 teaspoon fine salt
- ¼ of a whole nutmeg, ground
- ½ teaspoon ground cinnamon
- ½ teaspoon ground allspice
- 50g (2oz) caster sugar
- 1 x 7g (¼oz) sachet of dried yeast
- 100g (3½oz) currants
- Grated zest of 1 medium orange
- 150ml (¼ pint) hand-hot water
- 50ml (3½ tablespoons) hand-hot milk
- 1 large egg, beaten
- 50g (2oz) unsalted butter, melted (not sizzled – just melted)

Makes 12

For the topping
- 2 tablespoons plain flour
- 2 tablespoons water
- 1 tablespoon golden syrup, gently heated

Mix the ingredients
Measure the flour, salt, spices, sugar, yeast, currants and orange zest into a large mixing bowl. Mix and make a well in the centre.

Measure and combine the water and milk. Beat the egg and melted butter into the liquid.

Prepare the dough
Pour the liquid into the well in the flour mix. Use your hands to combine everything into a sticky dough. Turn it out and knead until smooth and elastic – about 5–10 minutes.

Rest the dough in the bowl for about 1 hour, or until it has doubled in size.

Make up the buns
'Knock-back' the dough to its original size and shape it into 12 equal sized balls. Place them on a lined baking tray and flatten them slightly with the palm of your hand. Cover and place in a warm place to rise for about 40 minutes.

Topping the buns
Meanwhile, for the topping, mix the plain flour with the water.

Preheat the oven to 220°C/425°F/ Gas Mark 7.

Gently pipe a cross onto each bun

When your buns have risen, put the flour and water mix into a piping bag and gently pipe a cross onto each bun.

Transfer the buns to the oven and bake for about 15 minutes, or until pale and golden.

Glaze the buns
Gently warm the golden syrup and as soon as you remove the baked buns from the oven (they will probably be touching each other), quickly brush the tops with the hot syrup.

Leave to cool on a wire rack, tear apart and eat fresh with butter. Delicious toasted as well!

HALLOWEEN

WHEN YOU MAKE A PUMPKIN LANTERN FOR THE KIDS, DON'T FORGET YOU CAN MAKE SOME DELICIOUS MEALS WITH THE FLESH. AND HALLOWEEN IS A GREAT EXCUSE FOR A PARTY (IF YOU NEED ONE!).

Tops tips for throwing a Halloween party

Halloween is more fun than spooky these days – unless you are scared of getting on the scales the following morning, after a night of great food and drink. It is the perfect evening for a party involving both children and adults.

1. Trick or treat?

If you are happy for trick-or-treaters to call – give them a sign, such as a pumpkin lantern in the window (and make sure your kids know the signs for others).

Remember – not everyone enjoys Halloween and trick-or-treating so only call at houses where you know your children will be welcome.

2. Personalized trick-or-treat containers

- Rather than spending money on plastic party bags, which eventually end up in the rubbish, save larger envelopes from your post, open carefully then paint with spooky designs.
- Hold onto old plastic jars and make simple handles out of string. Cut moons and stars out of yellow sticky labels and apply.
- Write the name of each child on their container – it will save tears later.

3. Ideas for making your house a little spooky

- Turn the lights down low.
- Put cobwebs on the windows made from black yarn.
- Get the children to make pipe cleaner spiders and dangle them from the ceiling.
- 'Build' a body as a table centrepiece using sheets, old clothes, wellington boots, tomato ketchup and peeled grapes for eyes.
- Make pumpkin lanterns – save the pumpkin flesh for our delicious recipes.
- Use yellow frieze paper painted with ghosts instead of a tablecloth.

4. Face painting

Masks are great but for young kids scared by some of the more ghoulish ones, try face painting on the night (even mum and dad can get involved). And you don't have to be Van Gogh… Here are some ideas to try:

Dracula Paint the face white, put a small drip of red paint on one side of the mouth, add arched black eyebrows and a pointed V-shape in a dark colour at the centre of the forehead where it meets the natural hairline.
Frankenstein Paint the face green, put a scar on one cheek and square off the natural hairline using dark face paint. Draw a bolt on the side of the neck.
Zombie Paint the face white. Smudge grey circles under the eyes. Paint the lips pale green or blue.

5. Spooky food

As well as the pumpkin recipes in this chapter, try...

Sausages cooked indoors or on the barbecue – serve with tomato ketchup in a small plastic witch's cauldron.

Or, for the adults, fill the cauldron with our 'Scarily Spicy Halloween Relish': dice a large tomato and half a peeled cucumber, then add three finely sliced spring onions, a deseeded medium heat or hot chilli, salt, black pepper and the juice of a lime.

6. And games!

Halloween pass the parcel Put spooky music on. Wrap the parcel as usual but use 'creepy crawly sweets', such as spiders and snakes.
Scary musical statues Everyone has to freeze in scary positions when the music stops. Judges can try to make them move but without touching participants.

Create a spooky glow

Kids love pumpkin lanterns but where do you start? There are lots of different ways to make them – you can keep it really simple or you can go wild. These instructions will give you the basics and your imagination can do the rest.

YOU WILL NEED

- 1 pumpkin
- Sharp knife, pumpkin carving tools or small drill
- 'Face' template (see **Templates** section)
- Pen or pencil
- Large spoon
- Bowls for the seeds and pulp
- Tealight

Make the lid

Using a sharp knife, cut a circular piece from the top of the pumpkin to form the lid.

Draw your design

Mark out your design in pencil or felt-tip pen on the pumpkin. You can do your own thing or use our template at the back of the book.

Scoop out the insides

Using a spoon, first scoop out all the seeds and put them into a bowl. If you plan to make pumpkin soup or pumpkin pie afterwards you will want to keep the seeds and pulp separate. Next scoop out the pulp – you won't be able to get it all out, but enough to clean it up inside.

Start cutting

This is the tricky stage and you will need to supervise any children using knives.

Start by cutting out the larger pieces first and then work up to the fiddly bits once you have had some practice. If you have a small drill tool you can get much more intricate.

Don't worry if you cut a piece you weren't meant to cut, just pin it back together with a toothpick later or create a new detail.

Light your lantern

Wipe the outside clean. Place the lantern in your chosen position, pop a tealight inside and you are ready to scare away the ghoulies and ghosties!

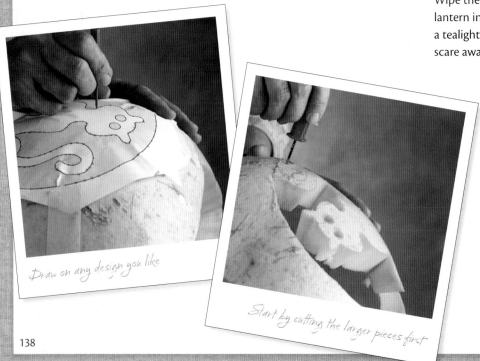

Draw on any design you like

Start by cutting the larger pieces first

Halloween trick-or-treat jars

Have some fun on the spookiest day of the year collecting treats in these decorated little jars. Or, use them with a tealight inside to make fantastic ghostly candles.

YOU WILL NEED

- Old jam jars – washed thoroughly
- PVA glue
- Paintbrush
- Coloured tissue paper
- Tealights (optional)
- Wire to make carry handles
- Acrylic paints (optional)

Decorate the jar

Paint some PVA glue onto the outside of the jar. Tear a piece of coloured tissue and gently glue it onto the jar. Repeat the process until you have covered the whole jar. You can cut out shapes such as pumpkins to paste on.

Make a handle

Twist some wire around the neck of the jar a couple of times and then make a loop for carrying the jar or hanging it up. Or you can just line them up on the mantelpiece or window sill.

Tip

Another option is to paint the jars using acrylics – spooky faces, witches and cats – or let the kids have their own ideas.

Pumpkin magic – 3 ways with leftovers

If you are carving pumpkins into spooky lanterns there are a number of ways to cook and serve their rich, sweet-tasting flesh. As well as the traditional orange pumpkin, try experimenting with different varieties, from the tiny yellow and green ones to 'Cinderella coach' giants.

Here are three ideas for pumpkin as a starter, main course and pudding. You can infinitely adapt these basic recipes.

Pumpkin soup

Use this basic recipe below but add in your own unique flavours, such as ground cumin, finely diced fresh chilli, or a cup of orange juice.

Garnish before serving with cream, soured cream or crème fraiche and some chopped green herbs, such as basil or parsley.

YOU WILL NEED

- 45ml (3 tablespoons) olive oil
- 1 large onion, chopped
- herbs/spices to taste
- 500g (1lb 2oz) pumpkin, peeled, deseeded and chopped
- 150g (5oz) potato, parsnip, or sweet potato
- 700ml (1¼ pints) vegetable stock
- salt and pepper
- fresh basil or parsley and soured cream or crème fraiche to garnish

Serves 6

Heat the oil in a large, heavy-based saucepan, add the onion and herbs or spices and cook over a moderate heat for 8–10 minutes until the onions have softened.

Add the pumpkin and your other vegetable, stir for a few minutes and then add the stock. Bring to the boil and simmer for 20–30 minutes or until the vegetables are tender.

Mash the mixture with a potato masher, or allow it to cool slightly and then blitz in a blender for a smoother soup.

Reheat the soup gently and add the orange juice if using. Season to taste and serve in warm bowls topped with fresh herbs and a spoonful of soured cream or crème fraiche.

Pumpkin stew

Ring the changes with pumpkin stew by varying the tinned beans you use – kidney, butter and berlotti are all good choices. Or use a combination.

Add garlic and/or chilli to vary the intensity and flavour. You can also add bacon pieces or lardons

Crumble in cheese just before serving – a crumbly blue cheese, Cheshire, or a sturdy cheddar all work well.

YOU WILL NEED

- 45ml (3 tablespoons) of olive oil
- 2 large onions, chopped
- 3 cloves garlic (optional), sliced
- 1 medium chilli (optional), deseeded and chopped
- approx. 200g (7oz) chopped bacon or lardons – depending on how meaty you want your stew
- 200g (7oz) potato, chopped
- 300g (11oz) pumpkin, peeled, deseeded and chopped
- 400ml (14fl oz) vegetable stock
- 2 x 425g (14oz) can of beans, rinsed and drained
- 200g (7oz) crumbly cheese (optional)

Serves 6

Heat the oil in a large, heavy-based saucepan, add the garlic, chilli, bacon or lardons if using and cook over

a moderate heat for 8–10 minutes until the onions have softened.

Add the potato and gently fry until slightly golden. You want the potato to develop a 'skin' so it holds its shape in the stew.

Add the pumpkin, fry it for a few minutes and then add the stock and the beans. Bring to the boil and simmer for 30–40 minutes. Don't let it get too dry or too mushy.

Just before serving add your choice of cheese.

Sweet pumpkin pie

For ease, you can buy a packet of ready-made pastry, or if you have time, count the saving and make your own.

YOU WILL NEED

- 300g (11oz) sweet shortcrust pastry
- 450g (1lb) pumpkin, peeled, deseeded and chopped
- 75g (3oz) caster sugar
- 175ml (6fl oz) double cream
- 2 teaspoons mixed spice
- 2 large eggs, beaten
- ½ teaspoon cinnamon, to garnish
- Cream, to serve

Serves 8–10

Pre-heat your oven to 200°C/400°F/Gas 6.

Roll out the pastry on a lightly floured surface and use it to line a 23cm (9in) flan tin.

To make the filling, steam the pumpkin until it is nice and soft, drain and lay it on several layers of kitchen roll to absorb any excess moisture.

Place the sugar, cream and mixed spice in a pan and bring to a boil.

Place the pumpkin in a blender, add the whisked eggs and heated cream mixture and whiz until smooth.

Carefully pour the mixture into the pastry case and bake for 10 minutes. Then reduce the oven temperature to 180°C/350°F/Gas 4 and cook for another 45 minutes until firm (but not too firm).

Allow it to cool but don't chill. Dust with the cinnamon powder and serve with cream.

Allow to cool before serving

Tip

Turn this into a savoury pie by using a non-sweetened pastry, taking out the sugar and spices, and adding salt and pepper to taste, as well as a cheese such as feta or Stilton when you add the mixture to the pastry case.

Knitting techniques

Casting on

To begin knitting, you need to work a foundation row of stitches and this is called casting on. There are several ways to cast on stitches and a cable cast-on method is described here.

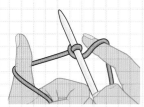 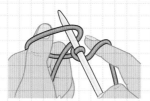 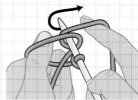 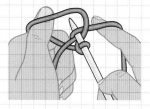

1 Take two needles and make a slip knot about 15cm (6in) from the end of the yarn on one needle. Hold this needle in your left hand. Insert the right-hand needle knitwise into the loop on the left-hand needle and wrap the yarn around the tip.

2 Pull the yarn through the loop to make a stitch but do not drop the stitch off the left-hand needle.

3 Slip the new stitch on to the left-hand needle by inserting the left-hand needle into the front of the loop from right to left. You will now have two stitches on the left-hand needle.

4 Insert the right-hand needle between the two stitches on the left-hand needle and wrap the yarn around the tip. Pull the yarn back through between the two stitches and place it on the left-hand needle, as in step 3. Repeat until you have cast on the required stitches.

Knit stitch

This is the simplest stitch of all. Each stitch is created with a four-step process. Hold the yarn at the back of the work – this is the side facing away from you.

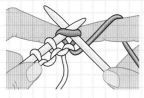 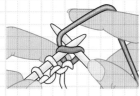 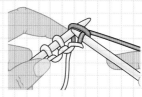 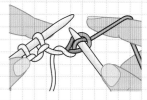

1 Place the needle with the cast-on stitches in your left hand, insert the right-hand needle into the front of the first stitch on the left-hand needle from left to right.

2 Take the yarn around and under the point of the right-hand needle.

3 Draw the new loop on the right-hand needle through the stitch on the left-hand needle.

4 Slide the stitch off the left-hand needle. This has formed one knit stitch.
  Repeat until all stitches on the left needle have been transferred to the right. Swap the right-hand needle into your left hand and begin the next row in exactly the same way.

Knit stitch – continental method

In this method the right-hand needle moves to catch the yarn; the yarn is held at the back of the work (the side facing away from you) and is released by the index finger of the left hand.

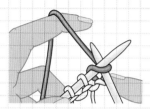  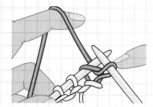 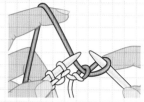

1 Hold the needle with the cast on stitches in your left hand and the yarn over your left index finger. Insert the right-hand needle into the front of the stitch from left to right.

2 Move the right-hand needle down and across the back of the yarn.

3 Pull the new loop on the right-hand needle through the stitch on the left-hand needle, using the right index finger to hold the new loop if needed.

4 Slip the stitch off the left-hand needle. One knit stitch is completed.

Purl stitch

This is the reverse of knit stitch. Hold the yarn at the front of the work – this is the side facing you.

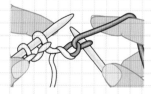 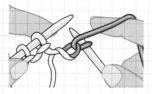  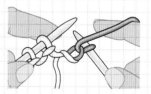

1 Place the needle with the cast-on stitches in your left hand, insert the right-hand needle into the front of the first stitch on the left-hand needle from right to left.

2 Take the yarn over and around the point of the right-hand needle.

3 Draw the new loop on the right-hand needle through the stitch on the left-hand needle.

4 Slide the stitch off the left-hand needle. This has formed one purl stitch on the right-hand needle. Repeat these four steps to the end of the row.

Purl stitch – continental method

Hold the yarn in the left hand, at the front of the work (the side facing you).

 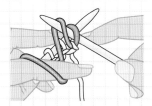 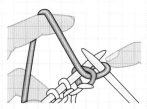 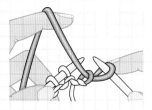

1 Hold the needle with the cast on stitches in your left hand and insert the right-hand needle into the front of the stitch from right to left, keeping the yarn at the front of the work.

2 Move the right-hand needle from right to left behind the yarn and then from left to right in front of the yarn. Pull your left index finger down in front of the work to keep the yarn taut.

3 Pull the new loop on the right-hand needle through the stitch on the left-hand needle, using the right index finger to hold the new loop if needed.

4 Slip the stitch off the left-hand needle. Return the left index finger to its position above the needle. One stitch is completed.

Increasing stitches

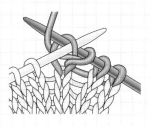

On a knit row Knit the first stitch on the left-hand needle in the usual way, but instead of sliding the stitch off the left-hand needle as you would normally do, still keeping the yarn at the back of the work, knit into the back of the same stitch. Then slide the stitch off the left-hand needle. You now have two stitches on the right-hand needle and have therefore created a stitch.

On a purl row Purl the first stitch on the left-hand needle in the usual way, but instead of sliding the stitch off the left-hand needle as you would normally do, still keeping the yarn at the front of the work, purl into the back of the same stitch. Then slide the stitch off the left-hand needle.

Decreasing stitches

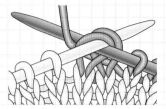 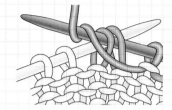

Decreasing one stitch – knit 2 together Knit to where the decrease is to be, insert the right-hand needle (as though to knit) through the next two stitches and knit them together as one stitch.

Decreasing one stitch – purl 2 together Purl to where the decrease is to be, insert the right-hand needle (as though to purl) through the next two stitches and purl them together as one stitch.

Binding off

Binding off (casting off) links and secures stitches together so that the knitting cannot unravel when completed. Binding off is normally done following the stitch sequence, so a knit stitch is bound off knitwise and a purl stitch purlwise. Don't bind off too tightly as this may pull the fabric in. To bind off on a purl row, follow the Bind Off Knitwise steps but purl the stitches instead of knitting them.

 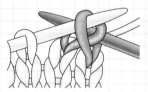 

Bind off knitwise
1 Knit the first two stitches. Insert the point of the left-hand needle into the front of the first stitch on the right-hand needle.

2 Lift the first stitch on the right-hand needle over the second stitch and off the needle. One stitch is left on the right-hand needle.

3 Knit the next stitch on the left-hand needle, so there are again two stitches on the right-hand needle. Lift the first stitch on the right-hand needle over the second stitch, as

in step 2. Repeat this until one stitch is left on the right-hand needle. Cut the yarn (leaving a length long enough to sew in) and pass the end through the last stitch. Slip the stitch off the needle and pull the yarn end to tighten it.

Darning in ends

You will have some loose ends from casting on, binding off and changing colours and these can be woven into the knitting to secure them and create a neat look. Thread the loose end through a large-eyed tapestry or darning needle and pass the needle through the 'bumps' of the stitches on the back of the work for about 5cm (2in) and then snip off excess yarn.

Sewing techniques

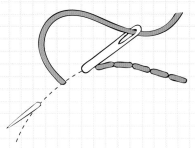

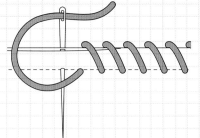

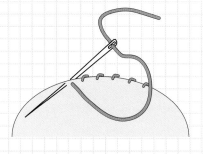

Backstitch

Backstitch is a very versatile stitch and can be used to 'draw' parts of a stitched motif, to add single stitches for emphasis and to outline areas.

Oversewing or Whip Stitch

This stitch is used to stitch two fabric edges together, particularly when sewing up gaps where quilts or other projects have been bagged-out through a gap. Fold the fabrics inwards to create folded edges and stitch together with matching thread and small stitches.

Slipstitch

This is simply tiny stitches used to secure fabric or trims in place and is really a hemming stitch.

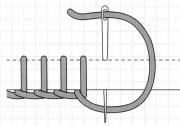

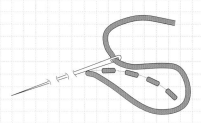

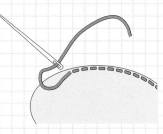

Blanket Stitch

This is the stitch most often used to edge appliqué motifs.

Running Stitch

This stitch is worked by taking the needle in and out of the fabric at regularly spaced intervals in any direction required.

Topstitch

This is usually done by machine but can be hand worked. It provides additional security on hemmed or folded edges and creates a neater, flatter edge.

DIY techniques

The projects in this book require only the most basic of DIY skills. Anyone willing to have a go should be able to do them without problems.

Project preparation

The best piece of advice is to assemble all the tools and materials you will need before you start. There is nothing worse than finding you are missing a screw when you have got something half attached to a wall and have to drop everything to find one or buy one.

Measuring up

The golden rule of DIY (and sewing!) is measure twice and cut (or drill) once. Mark where you need your hole with a pencil or felt-tip pen before you hammer or drill.

Surface preparation before painting

Don't cut the prep stage short. Time spent here saves time later and ensures a professional finish.

If you are going to be painting or varnishing, the surfaces need to be grease free. Use sugar soap from a DIY store for this or a good solution of washing up liquid. If the surface is glossy sand it down before re-painting, so the paint will stick to it. Do this lightly but thoroughly with a medium or fine sandpaper.

Protecting surfaces

Always use a cutting board when you are working with a craft knife. If you are working with a saw, make sure you don't saw through anything else. Borrow a work bench or use some bricks to support the wood away from other surfaces.

Use masking tape to mark off areas you plan to treat or paint and protect surrounding areas.

Working with a saw

Draw a guide line in pencil across the wood to show where you need to cut. Score along the guide line with a craft knife. Hold the saw with your index finger pointing to the blade.

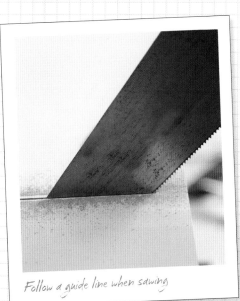

Follow a guide line when sawing

Start the cut by making a couple of backward strokes across the edge of the wood on the guide line. When you have a shallow groove you can begin to saw back and forward. Always use long strokes.

Most of the projects in the book need only a hacksaw.

Painting

Don't overload the paintbrush. To avoid leaving brush strokes, once you have painted, glide an unloaded brush or roller very lightly over the wet painted surface so you just skim it.

Drilling

The key to successful drilling is using the right drill bit for the job. See **Tools and equipment**. When drilling tiles (or plates) always use a piece of masking tape over the area to be drilled and mark the drilling spot on the tape with a felt-tip pen. Take care to wear gloves when changing drill bits – they can get very hot! If you're a DIY newbie, practice on a piece of spare wood until you are used to the feel of the drill in your hands and there is no risk of you jumping out of your skin when it starts going!

Templates

(All templates are shown at actual size,
except for Scotty dog doorstop)

Gift boxes for spring chickens

Score along dotted lines

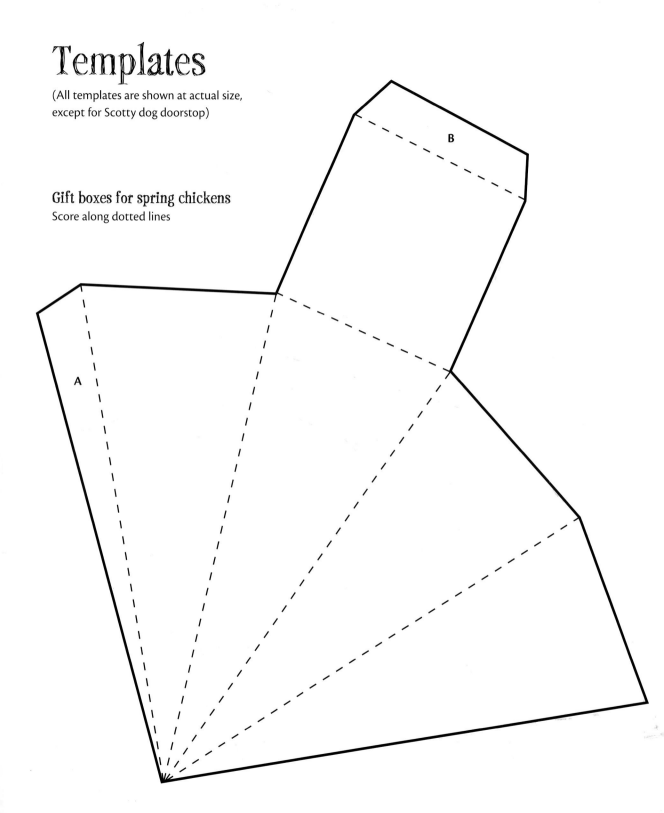

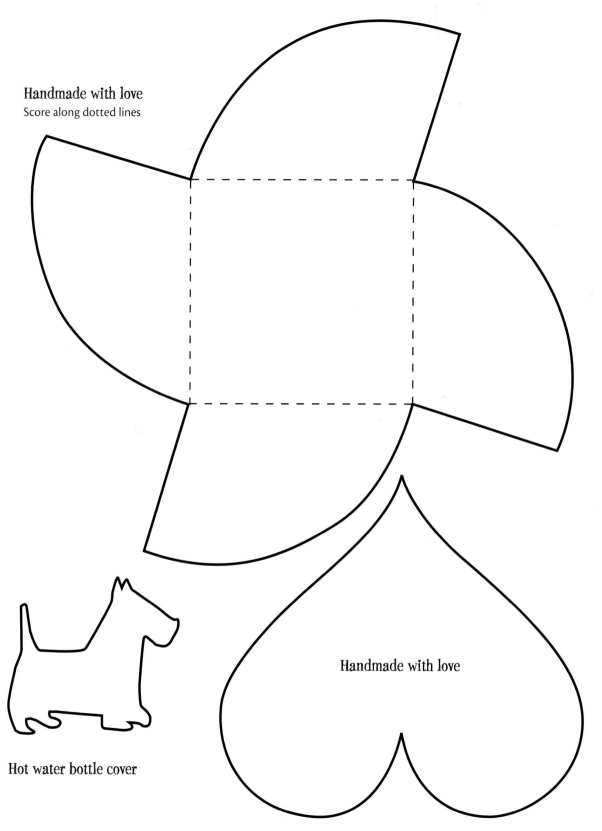

Handmade with love
Score along dotted lines

Handmade with love

Hot water bottle cover

153

Hop-along bunny tablecloth

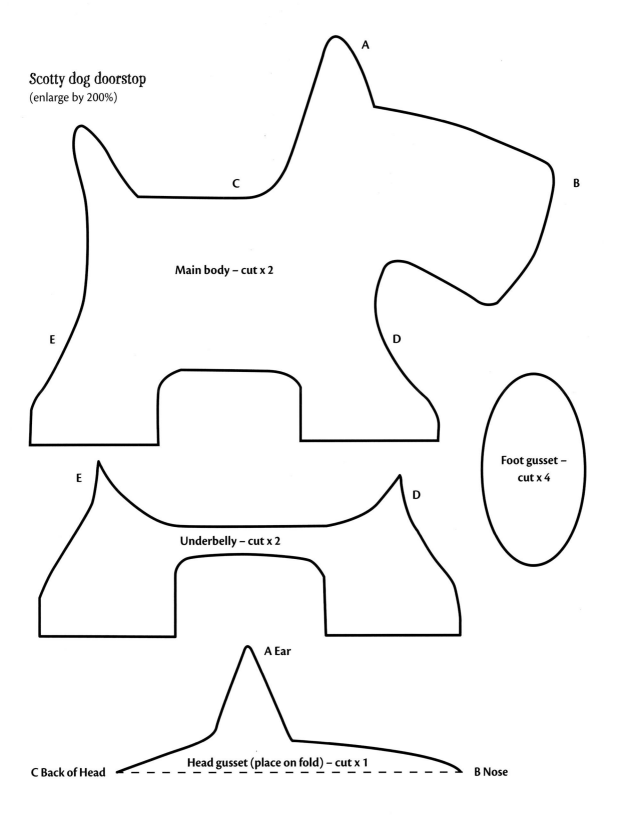

Scotty dog doorstop
(enlarge by 200%)

A

C

B

Main body – cut x 2

E

D

Foot gusset –
cut x 4

E

D

Underbelly – cut x 2

A Ear

C Back of Head

Head gusset (place on fold) – cut x 1

B Nose

Suppliers

RU Craft MIAMI Store

We've teamed up with RU Craft to create the perfect destination for most of your sewing, knitting, quilting and crafting needs. Plus fabulous fabrics for quilting, cottons and threads. And you can even buy your sewing machine there!
www.rucraft.co.uk/miami

Farrow & Ball

Farrow & Ball paint may cost a bit more but we think it is quite simply the best paint on the planet with the most fantastic range of colours and finishes. In the **Kitchen Cupboard Makeover** project we used their Incarnadine and Pitch Blue in Estate Eggshell and their undercoat and primer.

Buy online at www.farrow-ball.com or visit their showrooms.

Screwfix

Great for all things DIY. It is where the trade goes.
www.screwfix.com

DIY.com

B&Q's website. Great for home deliveries and DIY advice.
www.diy.com

Nigel's Eco Store

For a wide range of eco and energy saving products as well as helpful advice.
www.nigelsecostore.com

DIYTools.co.uk

An online shop for DIY tools and home improvement-related items.
www.diytools.co.uk

Amazon

Nine times out of ten you will find what you are looking for here – and the delivery is fast and efficient.

We used Amazon for the supports for the **Vintage Cake Stand**. Also great for cheap cushion pads and wadding (batting).
www.amazon.com

Lakeland

A good place for kitchen gadgetry – particularly for jams and preserves – they have everything from jam pans to labels and jars.
www.lakeland.co.uk

Jackson's Art Supplies

A great one stop shop for all things art related – brushes, paints, paper etc.

John Lewis

General haberdashery – if you don't have a local haberdasher.

eSpares.co.uk

For spare parts for virtually any appliance.
www.eSpares.co.uk

Dremel

Suppliers of a wide range of tools, glue guns and drills perfect for the keen crafter or DIY fiend.
www.dremel.com

But before you use any of these – ask yourself if there is something you can reuse, adapt or remodel. And for tools – don't buy it if you can borrow it! Remember it is the hole you want not the drill!

About the authors

Make it and Mend it was founded in 2009 by Clare Flynn, Hilary Bruffell, Clare O'Brien and Anne Caborn.

Clare F lives in West London where she writes novels and works as a management consultant. She loves painting and life drawing, sewing and quilting and is unofficial butt-kicker-in-chief for the MIAMI team.

Hilary, from Frensham in Surrey, isn't happy unless she's sewing up a cushion or restoring a piece of furniture. From knitting to growing peaches, she can do it and she's also our very own Dr Hilary as she's got a PhD in social psychology.

Clare O lives in Kew, where she's famed for her gourmet dinners, home-made sourdough and delicious preserves. She works in digital media, but likes nothing more than rolling her sleeves up and baking a cake or designing her own Christmas cards.

Anne lives and works in Brighton. She's the MIAMI DIY expert, happiest when she has a power drill in her hand. Anne likes nothing more than rooting about in skips and junk shops or prowling round her local recycling depot.

Acknowledgments

We'd like to thank:
Jill Sawyer for her (no longer) secret recipe for mincemeat, that she's refined over the years and which is now a firm favourite with her family and friends.

Robyn Astyl of Faithful to Nature in South Africa for showing us how to make perfume.

Jake Bruffell (who's inherited his mother's *Blue Peter* genes) for coming up with the coffee table from an old door.

Eileen Riddiford for her tried and tested sloe gin recipe and the hexagon brick barbeque.
April Masson and her friend Jemma for the idea of making a Christmas wreath from a wire coathanger.

All the team at our publishers F&W Media International for giving us the chance to do this book and making it look so beautiful – and the photographers Sian and Nick for their fab pictures.

And last but not least all the members of our growing MIAMI community for their support, ideas and boundless enthusiasm.

Picture credits

All photography unless otherwise listed below by Sian Irvine © F&W Media International Ltd.

p9 © Stock.xchng, p10 © istock/Наталья Ларина, p11 © living4media/ Christine Bauer, p12 © living4media/Heather Brown, p13 © Shopics/Alamy, p15 © Corbis Bridge/Alamy, p16 © Stock.xchng (bottom left), © Claudia Meyer, Paris, (centre), © istock/Matka Wariatka, p18 © istock/Matka Wariatka, p18 (top) & throughout © istock/hudiemm, p19 © dk/Alamy, p34 © istock/Pål Espenolsen, p36 © Stock.xchng (deckchairs © Gianluca Corderlina, daisies © OeilDeNuit), p36 (bottom left) & p40 © istock/Elena Rakhuba, p38 (bottom right) © Stock.xchng, p41 © istock/contact19, p43 © Getty/Lauri Rotko, p44 © Keith Morris/Alamy, p45 © Getty/PhotoLibrary/Michael Powell, p58 © Stock.xchng (middle left © bschwehn), p66 © Stock.xchng, p69 (right) © istock/ Dominik Pabis, (left) © istock/Peter Mukherjee, p74 © Stock.xchng, p76 © Food Photography Eising/StockFood UK, p77 © istock/1morecreative, p78 © Stock.xchng, p80 © ableimages/Alamy, p81 © Petr Gross/StockFood UK, p88 © Stock.xchng, p100 © Stock.xchng (pink roses © istock/Anna Omekhenko & p104), p110 © Stock.xchng (tulips © Sander Klaver) (middle right & p113 bottom © istock/Marie-France Cloutier), p112 © istock/kate_sept2004, p113 (top) © Clare Flynn, p115 © SciencePhotoLibrary/Alamy, p116 © istock/ temmuzcanarziray, p122 © Stock.xchng (Egg basket left & p124 © istock/ EllenMoran), p125 (bottom) © istock/Dean Mitchell, p134 © Stock.xchng (corn top centre © Thad Zajdowicz), p136 © living4media/Eising Studio-Food Photo & Video, p137 (top) © istock/Rich Legg, (bottom) © istock/Sean Locke, p138 © living4media/Krieg Roland, p139 © istock/Kenneth C.Zirkel, p142 © istock/Liliya Drifan, p143 © Ken Field/StockFood UK, p144 © istock/Lilyana Vynogradova, p145 © istock/Cameron Whitman, p151 © istock/Patricia Hofmeester

Index

A DAVID & CHARLES BOOK
© F&W Media International, Ltd 2012

David & Charles is an imprint of F&W Media International, Ltd
Brunel House, Forde Close, Newton Abbot, TQ12 4PU, UK

F&W Media International, Ltd is a subsidiary of F+W Media, Inc
10151 Carver Road, Suite #200, Blue Ash, OH 45242, USA

Text and Designs © Clare Flynn, Hilary Bruffell, Clare O'Brien and Anne Caborn 2012
Layout and Photography © F&W Media International, Ltd 2012, except those listed on page 157

First published in the UK and USA in 2012

Clare Flynn, Hilary Bruffell, Clare O'Brien and Anne Caborn have asserted their right to be identified
as authors of this work in accordance with the Copyright, Designs and Patents Act, 1988.

The author and publisher have made every effort to ensure that all the instructions in the book are
accurate and safe, and therefore cannot accept liability for any resulting injury, damage or loss to
persons or property, however it may arise.

Names of manufacturers and product ranges are provided for the information of readers, with no
intention to infringe copyright or trademarks.

A catalogue record for this book is available from the British Library.

ISBN-13: 978-1-4463-0240-8 hardback
ISBN-10: 1-4463-0240-7 hardback

ISBN-13: 978-1-4463-0292-7 paperback
ISBN-10: 1-4463-0292-X paperback

Printed in China by RR Donnelley for:
F&W Media International, Ltd
Brunel House, Forde Close, Newton Abbot, TQ12 4PU, UK

10 9 8 7 6 5 4 3 2 1

Acquisitions Editor: Sarah Callard
Editor: Jeni Hennah
Project Editor: Jessica Cowie
Designer: Prudence Rogers
Photographer: Sian Irvine
Senior Production Controller: Kelly Smith

F+W Media publishes high quality books on a wide range of subjects.
For more great book ideas visit: **www.rucraft.co.uk**